OUR STEWARDSHIP

Managing Our Assets

John L. Golv

D1275558

Augsburg Fortress
Minneapolis

Developed in cooperation with the Division for Congregational Ministries of the Evangelical Lutheran Church in America, Michael R. Rothaar, project manager.

This publication is designed to provide accurate and authoritative information in regard to the subject matter covered. It is sold with the understanding that the publisher is not engaged in rendering legal, accounting, or other professional services. If legal advice or other professional assistance is required, the services of a competent professional person should be sought.

Portions of chapter 4 and the chapter 4 tools are adapted from *Managing Risks, First Steps in Identifying Congregational Liability*, Richard B. Couser, copyright © 1993 Augsburg Fortress.

Series overview: David P. Mayer, Michael R. Rothaar
Editors: Laurie J. Hanson, Andrea Lee Schieber, James Satter

Cover design and series logo: Marti Naughton
Text design: James Satter
Cover photograph: Gordon Gray, FRPS

About the cover image: The centerpiece of the Resurrection Window in First Lisburn Presbyterian Church, Northern Ireland, was created by stained glass artist James Watson, Belfast, from fragments of church windows destroyed by a car bomb in 1981 and restored after a second bomb in 1989. The window symbolizes new life in Christ, which transforms darkness to light, hatred to love, despair to hope, and death to life. The members of First Lisburn Presbyterian have lived out this promise through new initiatives for community service, reconciliation, and peace-making.

ISBN 0-8066-4406-0

The paper used in this publication meets the minimum requirements of American National Standard for Information Sciences—Permanence of Paper for Printed Library Materials, ANSI Z329.48-1984.

Manufactured in the U.S.A.

06   4   5   6   7   8   9   10

✛ Contents

Series Overview

Welcome to the Congregational Leader Series, and welcome to the journey of discovering God's future for you and your congregation. Your congregation's mission and ministry are given to you by God. We sometimes refer to "our church," but it is always Christ's church. We are at best its stewards or caretakers, not its owners. As we plan, organize, and lead, we strive toward excellence in everything we do to reflect the glory and grace of God, who has entered human life to redeem us.

As a congregational leader, you may be asking, "What is our mission? How should we structure things? How can we plan for the future and where will the resources come from?" The Congregational Leader Series provides resources for effective planning and leadership development. Each book includes biblical and theological foundations for planning and leadership development, and practical information to use in building on your congregation's strengths.

We are first of all called to be faithful to God's word and will. Exploring the Bible enables us to discern what God's plan is for us as individuals and as a congregation. Ignoring or minimizing the centrality of God in our deliberations risks not only failure but also our faith. In the words of the psalmist, "Unless the LORD builds the house, those who build it labor in vain"(Psalm 127:1).

Why should we engage in congregational planning and leadership development? When the congregation is at its best, these activities aid us in fulfilling our mission to the world: reaching out with the gospel of Jesus Christ. Faithful planning for mission mirrors God's activity in the world, from creating and covenant-making to gathering and renewing the church. When congregations fail to plan, they risk dissipating the resources they have been given by God and begin falling away from all that God has intended for them.

In short, faithful planning and leadership development engage the congregation and all its members in the creative work of God. Continually analyzing and shaping our vision, mission, ministry, and context allows us to ask, "What is God calling our congregation to be?" Working to develop and support leaders enables us to ask, "How has God gifted each of us for ministry?"

We begin with prayer

As congregational leaders, we always begin our endeavors with prayer. Discerning God's will for us is a task that requires that we be in communication with God. Unfortunately, we often come up with new ideas and programs—and then pray that God will bless them! That order needs to be reversed. Our prayers should precede our plans, helping us discern God's call to us.

As congregational leaders, we always begin our endeavors with prayer.

In his few years of public ministry, Jesus accomplished a tremendous amount of healing, teaching, and service for others. However, his ministry did not begin until after he had spent an extended period of time in the wilderness reflecting on his call and God's purpose for his life. Following that retreat, virtually every moment of his life's story was punctuated with prayer and ultimately concluded with his supplications in Gethsemane and on the cross.

Paul wrote to the Thessalonians, "Rejoice always, pray without ceasing, give thanks in all circumstances; for this is the will of God in Christ Jesus for you" (1 Thessalonians 5:16-18). These words were meant for us—congregational leaders anxious to get on with things that need to be done. Notice how Paul places *prayer* between *rejoice* and *thanks* in this verse. Prayer is not simply another task to be done nor an obligation to be met. It is a gift of God to be celebrated and used with joy and thanksgiving. It is meant to permeate our lives. As leaders, we are seeking to construct God's will in our communities. God invites us to build with gladness and to make prayer the mortar between every brick we lay.

We build from strength

Most leadership resources begin with the assumption that there is a problem to be solved. In the midst of the real problems that surround us, however, our task as congregational leaders is to identify the strengths, giftedness, and blessings that God has given to us and the congregation. Our primary calling is not to be problem-solvers but to be asset-builders. Paul reminds us, "Let all things be done for building up"(1 Corinthians 14:26). This is not license to ignore problems, conflicts, or deficiencies. Rather, it is a call to view the brokenness around us in a new way.

Our primary calling is not to be problem-solvers but to be asset-builders.

Our role as Christian leaders is to attempt to look at our congregation, our fellow Christians, and ourselves, as God sees us. "This is my commandment, that you love one another as I have loved you" (John 15:12). Jesus did not blindly ignore the problems around him. Instead, he viewed those problems through a lens of love, appreciation, and forgiveness. We are called to build from strength, to construct our plans and visions from what God has given us. When we try to build from weakness and focus only on our problems, we compound both and ultimately fail.

First Church was located in a growing, well-to-do suburb, on a main thoroughfare, and in a beautiful new building. The members of First Church appeared to have everything going for them, and the congregation's future looked very bright.

The congregation, however, faced an ongoing problem with mortgage payments. This problem became so all-consuming that the congregation began to lose sight of its strengths, gifts, and mission for the future. The members of First Church had everything they needed to solve the problem of mortgage payments but they were unable to stop fixating on it. Soon, many other issues surfaced as everyone became a fault-finder.

Today there is no mortgage-payment problem because there is no First Church. The preoccupation with weakness and deficiency blinded the congregation to the reality of its gifts. This congregation died, not because of its problems but because of its perspective.

We must constantly ask ourselves and others, "Where is God at work here? What gifts have we received for ministry in this place?" Focusing only on what we don't have breeds jealousy, competition, hopelessness, and lost vision. Focusing on our gifts gives birth to joy, affirmation, and hope.

We won't find quick fixes

We live in a culture obsessed with quick fixes and mesmerized by the notion that there is a prescription for every ailment and accident. But things keep falling apart. People get sick. Programs fail. Committees don't function. Plans backfire. And goals aren't met. The list of mistakes, failures, misfires, and flops grows and grows. In his letter to the Romans, Paul reminds us that "all have sinned and fall short of the glory of God"(Romans 3:23). Paul says this not to weigh us down with despair, but instead to remind us that our salvation comes from God and not ourselves.

Faithful leaders have a deep respect for the reality of problems and obstacles. Things will always fall apart. That's why planning, assessing, goal-setting, leading, and visioning are ongoing processes, not quick fixes. As leaders, we need to know the nature of sin and publicly acknowledge its pervasiveness. Then we can lead, not with unhealthy fatalism, but with honesty, humility, and a sense of humor.

We are all ministers

As Christians, everything we do and plan is communal. We cannot plan unilaterally or devise strategies in isolation. To be sure, each of us has received salvation individually through baptism, but at that moment, through the water and the Word, we were united with the body of Christ. Even the gifts that God has given each of us are meant for the common good of all God's people: "To each is given the manifestation of the Spirit for the common good" (1 Corinthians 12:7).

In other words, each of us is a minister, whether pastor or lay person, and each of us is called to serve others. This is a radical departure from our culture's overwhelming emphasis on individual

Each of us is a minister, whether pastor or lay person, and each of us is called to serve others.

independence. The idea that we are all ministers and that as the church we minister as a community has tremendous implications for all of our planning and development efforts.

Leadership development is nothing more than equipping the members of the congregation so that they are strengthened for ministry: "The gifts he gave were that some would be apostles, some prophets, some evangelists, some pastors and teachers, to equip the saints for the work of ministry, for building up the body of Christ" (Ephesians 4:11-12). Paul would be appalled at the idea that a paid professional minister should carry out all of the ministry of the congregation or that only some people in the congregation are called to ministry.

Faithful planning and leadership development affirm that all of God's people are gifted and invited to participate in ministry. Identifying, embracing, and strengthening each other's gifts for common mission is a daunting task that never ends, but through that effort and in that journey we become what God intended: "But you are a chosen race, a royal priesthood, a holy nation, God's own people, in order that you may proclaim the mighty acts of him who called you out of darkness into his marvelous light" (1 Peter 2:9).

A model for understanding congregations

Congregations are extremely complex. Throughout the Congregational Leader Series, we invite you to look at your congregation through a particular model or set of lenses. This model helps us to understand why congregations are so complex, and it provides some important clues for the leadership skills and tasks that are needed.

A congregation resembles three different institutions at the same time: a *community of spiritual formation*, a *voluntary association*, and a *nonprofit organization*. This isn't a matter of size—the largest and smallest are alike in this. It isn't a matter of context—the model applies to both urban and rural settings. Each type of institution has different values and goals, which may even contradict each other. Each of these values and goals requires different things from leaders.

Communities of spiritual formation

A congregation is, in part, a community of spiritual formation. People come to such a community to join with others in growing closer to God. They seek to understand God's word and God's will for their life. They seek an experience of God's presence, a spiritual or emotional awareness of transcendence and love. They seek time for contemplation and prayer, and also time to work with others on tasks that extend God's love to others.

How are our congregations communities of spiritual formation? Much of congregational life centers on worship. We teach children and adults the practice of faith. The church provides support in Christ's name during times of crisis and need. We engage in visible and public activities, such as offering assistance to people who are homeless, or hungry, or survivors of abuse, as a way of both serving God and proclaiming God's mercy and justice.

The most important value in a community of spiritual formation is authenticity.

The most important value in a community of spiritual formation is authenticity. There is no room for pretense, no room for manipulation, and no room for power games. The goals we establish must be clearly directed to outcomes in people's spiritual lives. The fundamental question for self-evaluation is this: "How has our ministry brought people closer to God?"

Voluntary associations

Like any club or voluntary association, a congregation is a gathering of people who are similar to one another in specific ways, share a common purpose, and largely govern and finance their organization's existence and activities. In addition, people often find that belonging to a club is a way to make friends and social or business contacts, and enjoy meaningful leisure time activities. Some voluntary associations, such as Kiwanis or Lions clubs, have charitable purposes and sometimes seek support from people beyond their own membership. Some voluntary associations are focused on common interests or activities, such as gardening or providing youth athletic leagues.

Membership requirements may be strict or fluid, costs may be high or low, and commitments may be long or short, but they are spelled out rather clearly. A number of unwritten rules may serve to get people to conform to common values. Most voluntary associations would like to have more members, both to strengthen their organization and to expand the social benefits that come from a broader circle. But the new members usually are people who are very much like those who are already members.

The most important value in a voluntary association is effectiveness in helping people relate to one another.

The most important value in a voluntary association is effectiveness in helping people relate to one another. The goals are largely relational. There must be many opportunities for people to form relationships, especially with those with whom they have much in common. The association must operate in such a way that people all feel that their own values and hopes are being well served, usually through direct access to the decision-making process and ample opportunities for public dissent. People want and expect to be contacted regularly by both leaders and other members, and to feel that they are fully accepted as part of the group.

It is also important that there is a consensus—a shared vision—on what the association is and does. When conflict emerges, it must be negotiated and resolved. Because membership is voluntary, when there's conflict, or when they just don't feel part of the group anymore, people are usually quick to withhold their financial support or quit altogether.

Nonprofit organizations

As if it weren't complicated enough to be both a community of spiritual formation and a voluntary association, now consider that your congregation is also a nonprofit organization. It is a chartered or incorporated institution, recognized as a legal entity by the federal, state, and municipal government. A congregation can borrow and lend, sue and be sued. You as a congregation are accountable to society and responsible for following all applicable laws. Almost all congregations are property owners and employers. The congregation has formal operational procedures and documents (from your constitution to state laws) that dictate how you must make decisions and conduct your affairs. The usually unspoken but fundamental goal of a nonprofit organization is self-perpetuation, making sure that the institution will continue.

In this regard, congregations are similar to any business that offers services to the public. Being *nonprofit* simply means that the organization's assets can't be distributed to individuals or for purposes contrary to the charter. It doesn't mean that the congregation can't or shouldn't be run in a businesslike manner—or that it can't accumulate assets. The actual operation doesn't differ much from that of a profit-making business. In a nonprofit organization, the primary value is efficiency, or achieving the greatest results with the least possible expenditure of resources.

Another core value is continuity, with orderly systems that must be applied by anyone who carries out the organization's work. To reach financial goals, a nonprofit organization seeks voluntary contributions and often regularizes revenue through endowments and ancillary sources of income. Efforts are made to minimize costs without sacrificing quality. The organization also tries to build reserves to meet unanticipated circumstances and periodic needs (such as replacement of depreciating assets). Policies are in place to protect the staff and volunteers, and to ensure clear and mutually agreed upon expectations. There are clear lines of accountability and each person operates within a specified scope of decision-making.

Planning in a nonprofit organization includes making the best use of property and facilities. The property is seldom an end in itself, but the goal of leadership is always to maximize its usefulness. Other organizational goals revolve around having a truly public presence, including marketing effectively, identifying the needs and wants of a particular group of people, developing a product or service that addresses those needs, and informing the target group of its desirability and availability. Nonprofit organizations must do this as surely and skillfully as those in the profit sector.

In a nonprofit organization, the primary value is efficiency, or achieving the greatest results with the least possible expenditure of resources.

You may have heard that "you shouldn't be a manager, you should be a leader." This is unfortunate language, because management is part of leadership, and voluntary organizations need managers. How you analyze, organize, delegate, supervise, and evaluate the congregation's work is critical to its vitality.

Leadership

What does the word *leadership* really mean? Think of it as having three dimensions: *character*, *knowledge*, and *action*. *Character* permeates all three aspects of this model. Leaders have principles and try to live them out. In any of the three ways in which we're looking at congregations, leaders are honest, trustworthy, dedicated, caring, disciplined, and faithful to the core principles—and have many more virtues as well. Although everyone sins and fails, be clear that improvement is expected from all leaders.

It is not only character that counts. Leaders must also know things and do things. *Knowledge* and *action* can be developed. They can be learned in books and classes or from working with people who have expertise. Things we know from one part of our experience can be applied to other parts of our lives.

Applying the congregational model

The three-part model of congregations is helpful in exploring the different things that leaders must be, know, and do in a community of spiritual formation, in a voluntary association, and in a nonprofit organization.

Problems develop when the values, goals, and leadership styles appropriate to one part of the congregational model are mistakenly applied to one of the others. It is not wrong to value authentic spirituality, effective interpersonal relationships, and operational efficiency. There are times when each of these should be given the highest priority. Recognize that your congregation probably has emphasized one of these areas at the expense of the others, and plan your way to a better balance. Embrace the wonderful complexity of congregational life and ask God to move among us to change us and renew us and rededicate us to God's own purposes.

The Congregational Leader Series

This is one of several books in the Congregational Leader Series. The entire series seeks to build on the positive, basing your planning on assets rather than deficiencies, and to focus on outcomes, enabling your congregation to make a specific and definable difference in people's lives. The series has two sets: congregational planning and leadership development. Books in this series can be used in any order, so you can get started with those books that are most helpful for you and your congregation. The reproducible tools can be used with your council, committees, planning teams, leadership groups, and other members of the congregation. Visit www.augsburgfortress.org/CLS to download and customize these tools.

Faithful planning and leadership development take us on a journey, a pilgrimage, and an exploration of God's possibilities for you and your congregation. The Congregational Leader Series provides resources for your travels, as you seek God's will and guidance for you and your congregation.

This image of a cross indicates that further information on a topic appears in another book in the Congregational Leader Series.

Introduction

This book is about God's stewardship and our own. We can grow in faith and stewardship by examining personal experience, hearing Scripture, and searching out the reasons why we have received what God has given us. Growing in faith and stewardship brings satisfaction, joy, and contentment into our lives as Christians. This brings us to a new place to live, a new way of living.

This book is about God's stewardship and our own.

In this book, stewardship is something that can be experienced personally and recognized in others. Christian stewards receive, use, and offer God's gifts, according to the heart and mind of God.

The key stewardship question is this: "Why do we have what we have?" This is a question for individual leaders and congregation councils, committees, ministry teams, and task forces. How many stewardship teams does your congregation have? Every congregational team—stewardship, property, finance, worship, education, and so on—is a stewardship team.

The words *gift* and *asset* are used interchangeably in this book, although each has shades of meaning. A gift often refers to a spiritual gift, as listed in Galatians 5:22-23, Romans 12:6-8, and other biblical passages. Spiritual gifts are necessary to accomplish the work of God in the world. All congregations have these gifts.

An asset, on the other hand, can include physical resources as well as human characteristics possessed by members of your congregation. Physical assets include such things as your church building, grounds, and neighborhood. Human assets include your leaders' standing, credibility, and trustworthiness. All congregations have valuable assets.

Overview of this book

Chapter 1 looks at the biblical foundations for stewardship and God's choices, abundance, gifts, and wishes.

Chapter 2 discusses how to discover the assets in your congregation.

Chapter 3 looks at leadership, a necessary component of faithful stewardship.

Chapter 4 outlines essential aspects of church asset management.

Chapter 5 suggests ways to build faith and increase support in your congregation.

Chapter 6 names challenges to financial stewardship and suggests solutions for leaders.

Chapter 7 discusses the use of commercial and denominational stewardship materials.

Chapter 8 discusses the basics of endowment funds.

The concluding chapter gives a new vision for God's leading stewards. The last section of this book includes tools to help you develop and build on stewardship efforts in your congregation.

Acknowledgments

This book could not have been written without the support of stewardship leaders in the Division for Congregational Ministries of the Evangelical Lutheran Church in America. I am particularly grateful to colleagues Michael Meier, Nancy Snell, Michael Rothaar, and Bob Sitze, friend and mentor. I am grateful to the shared and deployed staff of this division whose wisdom is reflected throughout this book.

Above all, I am grateful to my wife, Cathy, and to my children, Michael, Sarah, and Chris, whose love, support, and patience continue to reveal God's abundance.

This book is dedicated to my parents, Loyal and Ruth Golv, Christian stewards whose example led me to faith in Christ.

JOHN L. GOLV

Chapter 1

A New Place to Live

Prayer and Bible study change hearts and
reveal the heart and mind of God.

We live our faith in the One who is coming soon. During the wait, pressing human needs are always with us. Some needs and some people are easier for us to see than others. During the wait, some questions press hard on Christian faith. This book asks one of them: Why do we have what we have? During the wait, fresh reflection on Scripture reveals God's generosity and our tasks as stewards. During the wait, Christian stewards lead. Growing in the knowledge of God gives us new motivation and confidence to act, new willingness and sanction to take risks, as well as the possibility of genuine contentment.

More than a temple talk

It all seemed predictable enough. It was a beautiful Sunday morning in October. The church was full. The nights were cool, school was well in session, and the fall stewardship program began at church. The new chairperson stood up to deliver the first temple talk of the season. He started with one of Jesus' parables:

For it is as if a man, going on a journey, summoned his slaves and entrusted his property to them; to one he gave five talents, to another two, to another one, to each according to his ability. Then he went away. The one who had received the five talents went off at once and traded with them, and made five more talents. In the same way, the one who had the two talents made two more talents. But the one who had received the one talent went off and dug a hole in the ground and hid his master's money. After a long time the master of those slaves came and settled accounts with them. Then the one who had received the five talents came forward, bringing five more talents, saying, "Master, you handed over to me five talents; see, I have made five more talents." His master said to him, "Well done, good and trustworthy slave; you have been trustworthy in a few things, I will put you in charge of many things; enter into the joy of your master" (Matthew 25:14-21).

God's choices are at the heart of the Bible.

The chairperson got a chuckle by saying that we may not like the "slaves" part. He went on to say that we had done well. The previous year we not only made the budget, we also realized a needed increase in our income. "Well done," he said. We liked that part. He spoke for a few more minutes about the coming year.

I didn't hear much of the temple talk after the Bible passage. What I heard in that passage was not about me at all. In fact, what I heard had nothing to do with how well I had done or how good and trustworthy I had been. What I heard instead was what the master had done.

Jesus' parable of the talents begins with the master's choice to invest all that wealth in his slaves and leave them in charge. The parable ends with what the master expected the slaves to do with this wealth. In other words, the parable is about God.

Biblical stewardship

Biblical stewardship is not about *me first, my giving, my choices,* or *my faithfulness.* Biblical stewardship is about God's choices, God's abundance, God's gifts, and God's wishes. Shouldn't we start there?

God's choices

Biblical stewardship is no less than a matter of faith because it refers us first to God. We may be inclined to start with other urgent but less important matters close at hand, such as our church's needs. But if we start there, biblical stewardship becomes a secondary matter, something important only once a year, having little to do with faith. God's choices are at the heart of the Bible.

Biblical stewardship raises the stakes. It moves us from a once-a-year church budget emphasis to an emphasis on faith. God's choices are at the heart of the Bible.

> " The somewhat unexpected biblical testimony is to God's stewardship, first and foremost, rather than ours."
>
> —John Reumann, *Stewardship and the Economy of God* (Eerdmans, 1992), p. 118.

God's abundance

Could this happen at your church? The pastor stands up for announcements and begins by saying, "There are far too many people in church today. That is going to be a problem because there is only enough forgiveness for about one-third of you. I can see from here that many of you are in no way worthy to be in church today, much less hear the Word and receive the Sacrament. You know who you are. The ushers will see you out now. Come back next week if you haven't sinned so much. Then it may be that there will be enough forgiveness to go around."

Christian worship could never start this way, could it? With God, there is no question of limits or short supply. With faith we see what the prodigal son saw (Luke 15:11-32), that God is generous with us well past what we deserve, all for love. We have received grace upon grace (John 1:16) and our cups are running over (Psalm 23:5).

God's abundance is at the heart of the Bible.

Jesus' life, death, and resurrection show that God does not withhold anything. Jesus taught that God's kingdom is worth any price (Matthew 13:44-45). God is the generous father of the prodigal son and the gracious vineyard owner who hired workers even at the end of the day, whose generosity was not to be begrudged (Matthew 20:1-16). God knows and supplies what we need. There is enough forgiveness to go around, and no sinner is ever turned away.

When we focus on scarcity, it seems as though there isn't enough of anything, that God hasn't been generous. As a result, our faith shrinks down to what little can be seen. But with faith we can see abundance, far more than enough. Once we become aware of God's abundance, we may also realize that there is more than enough of all God's gifts. God's abundance is at the heart of the Bible.

God's gifts

Seeing God's abundance leads to two questions on faith matters. The apostle Paul raises the first question in 1 Corinthians 4:7: "What do you have that you did not receive?" This question is not meant to be answered, since the answer is obvious when we see God's abundance. The second question, also a faith matter, is not obvious, and is meant to be answered: Why do you have what you have?

We have what we have to use well. Gifts that seem ordinary to some people may seem priceless to others. Your gift with children is not accidental. Why do you have it? Your ability to inspire and lead others is more than a family trait—it's a gift. Your imagination, your ability to see past the obvious—these are gifts. Your willingness to work, persevere, and change with the times are gifts, too. Why do you speak so well or write so well? Why do you work so hard to build up the church? These gifts are part of God's abundance, given to you and to your community. God's gifts are at the heart of the Bible. Can you see God's purpose in the gifts that you have?

God's gifts are at the heart of the Bible.

God's wishes

God's wishes are knowable. We can search the Bible to gain knowledge of God. This knowledge helps us to see what God wants. We have what we have so that we bear fruit. In the conclusion of the parable of the sower, Jesus said, "But as for [the seed] in the good soil, these are the ones who, when they hear the word, hold it fast in an honest and good heart, and bear fruit with patient endurance" (Luke 8:15).

We have what we have so that we build up the church. There are many spiritual gifts. Galatians 5:22-23 lists the gifts of love, joy, peace, patience, kindness, generosity, faithfulness, gentleness, and self-control. In Romans 12:6-8, these gifts include prophecy, ministry, teaching, exhortation, generosity, diligence, and cheerfulness.

We have what we have so that we wait well. In 1 Corinthians 1:4-7, Paul writes: "I give thanks to my God always for you because of the grace of God that has been given you in Christ Jesus, for in every way you have been enriched in him, in speech and knowledge of every kind—just as the testimony of Christ has been strengthened among you—so that you are not lacking in any spiritual gift as you wait for the revealing of our Lord Jesus Christ."

Luke 12:48 refers directly to God's expectations of how we handle the things entrusted to our care: "From everyone to whom much has been given, much will be required; and from the one to whom much has been entrusted, even more will be demanded." This verse is part of a larger discussion on how well Christ's stewards wait for his return.

The stewards were expected to know what the master wanted. They were excused if they did not know the master's wishes and punished if they did know and did nothing (Luke 12:47-48).

In the parable of the talents (Matthew 25:14-30), a man leaves his investments with three slaves and goes on a journey. When the man returns, we find that he clearly expected to see a return on his investments—and expected the slaves or stewards to know this.

God's wishes are summarized in Micah 6:8 in this way: "what does the Lord require of you but to do justice, and to love kindness, and to walk humbly with your God?" In addition, 1 Timothy 2:4 points out that God "desires everyone to be saved and to come to the knowledge of the truth." God's wishes are at the heart of the Bible. What does God want you to do?

> **God's wishes are at the heart of the Bible.**

In the essay "Stewardship in the Teachings of Jesus," author Warren A. Quanbeck said that our relationships to our neighbors are "precisely the place where faithfulness to Christ is to be exercised. The person in need of food, clothing, hospitality, or care is Christ to the disciple."

In a comment crucial to knowing the will of God, Quanbeck went on to say, "Jesus' standard may be summarized: absolute attachment only to absolutes, relative attachment to relative values. But the relative values are to be taken seriously, for they are the test of loyalty to God."

From *Stewardship in Contemporary Theology*, edited by T. K. Thompson. (Association Press, 1960, p. 52).

Overwhelming gratitude

Giving thanks to God is one of the main themes of the Bible. Gratitude results from the knowledge of God and goes to the heart of our faith in God. God calls us to grow and mature in faith. One of the best ways to grow spiritually is to pray gratefully and live out our thanks to God.

There are no limits to God's gracious giving.

People who recognize God's abundance are overwhelmed with the need to give thanks. Gratitude moves us to a new way of living. We may find that nothing is more urgent, more important, more consuming, more satisfying, or more faithful than praying prayers of thanks to God who gives so abundantly to us, all for love.

A new place to live

It may seem now that the first reality in the new place is God. It is. Living life in this new place of gratitude honors God above everything else. Christian life as a steward means growing in the knowledge of God and discovering that God is made known in what God gives. This is an ongoing spiritual experience and a substantial part of the joy in living a Christian life.

It now may seem that there is far more blessing near at hand than you have ever seen before. It may seem that God's generosity is often in plain sight, yet beyond our expectations and beyond what we can see at a glance, one-sided in the extreme. It is.

Christian life as a steward means becoming aware of God's abundance. Looking around the new place we can see that there are no limits to God's gracious giving. Living life in the new place of gratitude allows us to see what God values most and is willing to give.

New questions

It now may seem that searching out the reasons for why we have what we have is a pressing matter in the life of a Christian steward. It is. Christian life as a steward means seeing that there is far more that we can do, more than we ever knew before. God's expectations are in plain sight. It may seem that there are more people, more needs, and more opportunities to live our faith than there ever were before. There are. Living life in the new place of gratitude allows us to see reasons for why we have what we have.

When do we have enough to be happy?

New gratitude

Gratitude is a way of life for Christian stewards. Christian life as a steward means living with joyful experiences of thanksgiving to God. In gratitude we can see that God entrusts us with everything needed to accomplish God's purposes in the world. Living life in the new place of gratitude allows us to see past ourselves.

Contentment

Life in the new place is new because it allows us to have genuine contentment. When do we have enough to be happy? Many of us are tempted to say "never." There will always be some personal indulgence masquerading as a real need, so that we think life is incomplete and less than fully satisfying without it.

When do we have enough to be happy? The Christian response is that we already have more than enough to be happy, because God has blessed us. Paul says, "I have learned to be content with whatever I have. I know what it is to have little, and I know what it is to have plenty. In any and all circumstances I have learned the secret of being well-fed and of going hungry, or having plenty and being in need" (Philippians 4:11-12).

Summary

- Christian stewards receive, use, and offer God's gifts, according to God's plan.
- Christian life as a steward means living in gratitude, growing in the knowledge of God, and experiencing true contentment.

Chapter 2

New Gifts, New Assets

God is more active in every congregation
than any one member can see.

Until we look, we don't see them. They're worshipers in church to give thanks, to hear what God is doing, and to learn what God expects. They're CEOs, taking pride in paying their workers well and doing all they can to avoid layoffs. They're assistant managers in the back of the grocery store, making sure that overstocked food gets to food shelters. They're business people speaking personally about addiction recovery at the local prison. God's stewards are all around us.

Biblical images can help us recognize God's stewards. The slaves in the parable of the talents were aware of their master's expectations. Christian stewards strive to know God's expectations and act on that knowledge, recognizing that they are following a plan that is not their own, with resources not their own but entrusted to their care. They know that they are accountable for what they do with what they have. Stewards are not the owners but they also are not merely followers who do no more than what they are told. Stewards are trusted managers who act, who know why they have what they have.

Stories of faith and stewardship

I had been elected to serve on a team of people growing in their faith and leading a ministry that mattered to them and the congregation. It was my first meeting and I expected us to discuss tasks to be done and decisions to be made. Dick was the chairperson. "We do whole-life stewardship work on this team," he said. "Some of that means taking care of tasks and decisions, but most of the work is different. Tonight we will spend important time getting to know each other. I'll start."

Dick said that he had been raised in a Christian church. "Church was a way of life in our small town," he said. "It took me a while to realize that it wasn't church that affected everything in my life, though it certainly seemed that way. I realized later that it was my faith in God that affected everything in my life. I grew up thinking that our family never had enough—that's how it seemed to me. But I remember how thankful my parents were. They seemed more thankful than they had reasons for! They lived as though they had everything they wanted, even more than they wanted. It took me some time to see that was how they really felt. I now see that gratitude to God and content-ment in life can be powerful witnesses to faith. That is what I bring to this group."

Dick motioned to the person on his right. That was Charleen, a woman in her mid-20s. She spoke about how powerful the biblical image of the church as the body of Christ was to her. "It's not just talk," she said. "Our church is the body of Christ. We build each other up, and we act as Christ for the people who are on the margins. No one is left alone. I have realized how much our church can give to people who need help. That's what I bring to this group."

The pastor was next. "I bring my public witness," he said. "As you know, I preach the texts, even the hard ones. Jesus had a lot to say about what we do with what we have. Part of my witness is my giving. My family and I have worked our way up to tithing. I say this publicly once a year, so I guess you could say that I preach what I practice."

"I preach what I practice."

Recently retired from the public-school system, Carol had been a member of the congregation for many years. She spoke of her journey. "When I started teaching in the public schools," she said, "there was only so much that a woman could say and still be heard. There were limits to how far a woman's career could advance. I discovered that limits can be moved or removed and ended my teaching career in a leadership position. That's what I bring to this group."

"I don't actually know why I'm here," Darrel said. "I've probably been on too many committees. I'm too blunt, too opinionated, and too old for any of this."

Then Dick responded, saying, "Darrel, you are also one of the best communicators in our church. When you talk, people listen, and when you're done, they understand what was said. That's what you bring to our group."

Next, it was my turn. I said, "I haven't been part of a church leadership team before. I haven't been a member here for very long. But I have had some experiences in my life which have shown me what matters most. And they are what I will bring to this group." Stories like these are assets in a leadership team and assets in a congregation.

> God is more active in every congregation than any one member can see.

Discover what you have

The assets that you and others bring to a team often can be communicated as personal stories. Bear in mind that humble people often minimize their valuable assets. Some assets may even be hidden from the people who possess them.

Discovering the assets on your team and in your congregation is a group effort. No one sees all of God's abundance. There is more to your team and your congregation than one person can see. God is more active in every congregation than any one member can see.

God gives everything we need to do appropriate ministry where we live. We have more capacities than we think, more willingness, more confidence, more awareness, more openness, more of everything that is needed to carry out our mission.

Physical assets

Some people are gifted with knowledge of physical assets and can give complete answers when asked about what the congregation owns. The property team may be aware of the land, building, utilities, roof surfaces, windows, asphalt, heating and air conditioning, carpeting, furniture, audio-visual equipment—everything physical.

A comprehensive inventory of your congregation's physical assets should be completed every few years. The team in your congregation that deals with property, finance, or management might lead this effort. In addition to showing what God has given the congregation, an inventory of physical assets can be helpful for ensuring adequate insurance coverage and dealing with depreciation. An inventory like this is a snapshot of the value of the congregation's physical assets. The results may be surprising.

Spiritual assets

The team in your congregation that deals with stewardship, worship, or evangelism might undertake a periodic inventory of spiritual assets. These are not easily counted, but well worth the time and effort to identify. This list would include God's gifts of the Bible, people of faith, experiences of forgiveness and salvation, and stories of changed lives.

See "More Than Enough" on pages 82-89.

Assets received over time

Some people can speak of assets given by God over time. There was leadership when leadership was necessary. There were reliable workers, teachers, motivators, and subtle diplomats. There were visionary leaders who saw clearly what could be—and helped bring it about.

An asset inventory

A comprehensive inventory of your congregation's assets can demonstrate how much of extraordinary value has been entrusted to the congregation. Use the "More Than Enough" tool to do an inventory of the assets on your team and in your congregation. Once you start listing everything that your congregation is involved in, it may be hard to stop. Your congregation's assets may be far broader and deeper than you know. There is probably no one in your group who is aware of everything your congregation is doing. Even long-time members may learn about something new.

Your congregation's assets may be far broader and deeper than you know.

Members of one congregation were surprised at the results of their asset inventory. Several of the congregation's assets were well-known, such as a strong tradition of excellence in caring for young children, genuine and visible expressions of compassion for those in need, meaningful worship, members with differing political views, and a history of service and mission. The inventory also uncovered several new assets: the children's ministry, many retired people interested in teaching, people who were working or had worked for city government, six professional and 18 amateur auto mechanics, two ham-radio enthusiasts, 14 people who changed careers and made a significant move while in their 50s, people who had seen opportunities and needs and worked to meet them, and a willingness to change in the interest of faithfulness.

Members of the congregation found that there were more assets and opportunities for ministry than any one member could see. These results sparked imaginations and started wide-ranging, positive conversations.

We never talked like that before

How does your church talk to itself? Are there words and phrases that come up often? Is the offering during worship services *received* or *taken*? The plate is handed down the row and it is in everyone's hands for only a moment before it is passed on. What is happening in that moment? For some people it is giving, an act of worship. For many it is not giving, but paying the church's bills.

Words reflect habits of thought and belief.

The difference between *paying* and *giving* can be the difference between life in the old place and life in the new place of gratitude. Bills are paid. Gifts are given and received. Paul did not write that "God loves a cheerful payer" but "God loves a cheerful giver" (2 Corinthians 9:7). An offering is a gift.

Words reflect habits of thought and belief. Long-held beliefs may be enshrined in language that everyone knows and uses regularly. How we talk is an important clue to what we believe. In some congregations the language most commonly used may speak of scarcity, not abundance: "We don't have much. We don't have what others have. Most have more than we do." If we talk about never having enough of anything, always lacking something, then we will feel justified in saying that we are deprived in some way. If we say everything is in short supply, low expectations are justified. If we don't have much, we can't do much. Over time this kind of talk can become persuasive, convincing, and even become accepted as truth.

See "How We Talk around Here" on pages 90-91.

It may be that everything needed really is available but people still talk as though things are short. Individuals and congregations can overlook God's abundance, even when everything needed is available in good supply. Recognizing God's abundance changes our vocabulary from one of scarcity and low expectations to one of thankfulness and God's expectations. Discover what vocabulary your congregation uses with the "How We Talk Around Here" tool.

Moving a congregation to a new place

As an individual and as part of a team, you can help your congregation move to a new place of gratitude. Part of your leadership is a matter of how you talk.

Part of your leadership is a matter of how you talk.

Use language that speaks about God's gracious giving and people will begin to realize the new reality all around them and offer prayers of thanks. Language about how little we have can only be discredited and replaced by language about God's abundance. Help to bring that about and maintain a language of gratitude by the way you talk.

Summary

- Asset inventories are tools to identify the gifts God has given.
- Recognizing God's abundance changes our vocabulary from one of scarcity and low expectations to language of thankfulness and God's expectations.

Chapter 3

God's Leading Stewards

Christian stewards can be faithful and effective
leaders in their congregations.

It's a basic human conflict. On the one hand, it is hard not to want to please everyone. When everyone is happy, leadership is easy and the approval rating is high. However, decision-making is difficult, and some decisions will not please everyone.

If what we want is what matters most, then what God wants will not come first. In that case, following the wishes of the majority will appear to be the leader's most important task. When this happens, congregations might even reach consensus too soon, without considering all of the options, with too little to show for all their gifts. Leadership, like stewardship, starts with God.

God's gift of leaders

God blesses every congregation with leaders. John P. Kotter and Gilbert R. Rendle, both authors of books on leadership, have made a distinction between visionary leaders and managers. For more information, see John P. Kotter, *Leading Change* (Harvard Business School Press, 1996) and Gilbert R. Rendle, *Leading Change in the Congregation: Spiritual and Organizational Tools for Leaders* (Alban Institute, 1998).

In brief, visionaries see past limits that can be moved or removed. Managers, on the other hand, see practical matters and how visions can be implemented with realistic numbers. Congregations need the leadership of both types of leaders.

Some Christian stewards are leaders who rally the congregation. The gifts of these leaders are well used in:

- seeing beyond the present situation
- determining significant groups
- determining gifts in groups
- defining shared causes
- building support with existing leaders
- rallying the congregation and asking for support
- leading by example
- serving others
- cultivating and training new leaders

Congregations need the leadership of both types of leaders.

What if these visionary leaders dominate in a congregation, or the congregation supports only visionary leadership? People may believe that all the serious work is done once a vision is clear. It may be that whatever does not relate somehow to the work of visioning will not even be considered. Those with the gifts of visionary leadership might have the final word, and the congregation will suffer, being over-led and under-managed. Without the gifts of management, even the most faithful vision may not last or be fully realized.

Some Christian stewards are leading managers. The gifts of these leaders are well used in:

- providing information for planning
- organizing
- ensuring accurate accounting
- guaranteeing donor intent
- monitoring budget compliance
- assuring financial stability
- leading by example
- serving others
- cultivating and training new leaders

What if these managing leaders dominate a congregation or if a congregation supports only this type of leadership? If leaders insist on one aspect of management (such as maintaining stability) at the expense of all others, it may be that nothing new can be considered because it might disturb stability. Those with the gift of management might have the last word, but the congregation will suffer, being over-managed and under-led. Without the gifts of visionary leadership, visions can be stifled, and maintenance of stability may be the only course of action, even when change is required.

Visionaries wish to "get on with it," believing that the strength of the vision is all that is needed for success. They may proceed too quickly. Managers see that organization and planning are important for success. They may proceed too slowly.

Cultivate leadership from groups

There are many groups within your congregation. Some groups are obvious and represent reliable sources of support for the leadership, programs, and ministries of the congregation. The most visible groups include:

- current leadership
- current members of teams or committees
- former leadership and team or committee members
- current and former volunteers
- established organizations within the congregation

These groups are fairly easy to convene, and their gifts may be well-known. Visionary leaders and managers come from these groups.

Some people in the congregation often see stark differences between congregational practice and Christian faith. These people may see how relatively un-demanding church involvement is, and how completely demanding Jesus is. There are some people who are always willing to go the extra mile, who are always willing to put their schedule aside, who make time even when they little time to spare.

These more unconventional groups may be:

- current and former Bible study leaders
- people who have seen poverty first hand
- people whose lives have been dramatically changed by the ministry of a congregation
- those who see diversity missing in the congregation

These people often affirm the positive in what is happening while pushing for more. They may not be represented on leadership teams. They may be harder to convene because they do not constitute easily visible groups. There may be a leader among them who can rally these people.

Cultivate leadership and seek representation from the groups within your congregation. The members of these groups have distinct gifts to share.

Change dynamics

Pleasing most of the people most of the time is often the highest priority for leaders, but there is more to leadership than this—especially for people entrusted with God's gifts. According to author Gilbert Rendle: "In a time when the environment is changing rapidly both inside and outside the congregation—when the very makeup of the congregation as well as the surrounding community and culture are changing—the focus on happiness and satisfaction is insufficient and, in the end, damaging" (*Leading Change in the Congregation*, Alban, 1998, p. 13).

God's gifts come with the expectation that they will be used for God's purposes. True joy is discovered in receiving, using, and offering God's gifts as stewards. This may require change in individuals and congregations. Even those people most certain that nothing more is required than what has always been done in the past can be motivated to learn what God requires of us and work to carry through faithfully with what we have been given.

Why do we have the building we have, on the corner we have it, with a changing neighborhood all around us? Are we to use these assets to maintain the ministry we once had with the previous neighborhood? Or can leaders see strong traditional assets as opportunities, even as God's call, to expanded mission? Our location in a changing neighborhood may be an asset and an undiscovered advantage. It may be that we are perfectly located to minister to people new to the church. Adding a new worship service for people living in the neighborhood may be a good use of location, which has always been understood to be an asset for mission.

Why do we have the endowment we have? Why do we have the community leaders that we have? Why do we have people so willing to work in programs or ministries that no one in our congregation has ever been involved in before? God has in fact blessed us with an abundance of faith, intelligence, judgment, ability, leadership, nerve, meaning, purpose, time, money, and all manner of opportunities for faithful use and giving.

What we have may be a starting point to show us what God is calling us to do. If the need for change and the reasons for change are compelling enough to motivate people to move beyond complacency, pain may be one of the first results. This can be heard in objections such as, "Our doors have always been open to anyone who wants to come to our church" and "The endowment is our best insurance."

Pain may be one of the first results of new ministries, even when they are begun for the right reasons and in the right way. Members of a congregation may feel grief in leaving behind what was a faithful way of life in favor of a new, equally faithful way of life. Leaders who are able to show how a new vision for ministry is faithful and workable may gain a following.

What does God want?

When making decisions, it is tempting to start with ourselves and what we want, but we should seek to start with God. This takes practice, but congregations are blessed with gifts to do what God wants. We do this by concentrating on what God gives and offering gratitude for what we would not otherwise have.

What is promoted as being what God wants is often nothing more than what the majority, minority, or a manipulative leader wants. These efforts will never go away. Neither will the question "What does God want?"

This is an insistent question. It demands answers. For Christian leaders there is no direction, no preferred future, and no plan without the effort involved in gaining knowledge of God. Members of a congregation may or may not welcome the effort involved. Our knowledge of God will always seem temporary and inadequate. There are no easy, faithful answers that will persuade most people most of the time.

It must also be said that God's revelation is not so murky that it is impossible to know God and what God wants. Some answers are clear. We are to do justice, feed and clothe people in need, love others, and lead by serving. Be prepared! You may discover what God wants from you. What you discover may seem expected or surprising, welcome or unwelcome, socially appropriate or inappropriate.

Congregations are blessed with gifts to do what God wants.

What does God want?

The witness of exemplary leadership

Good leaders are bold enough to propose that, after listening and reflection, *this* is what we propose that the congregation consider, as reasons why we have what we have. Having discovered where valuable assets lie, leaders go on record, make proposals, and take stands. Leadership by example is effective, a good use of God's gifts, and a way to experience growth in faith.

Leaders outside the congregation

Visionary leaders and leading managers allow others to suggest how the gifts of a congregation may be well used. One way to do this is to invite people who represent a particular ministry (Bible camps, for example) to suggest how your gifts might be used in support of what they are doing. These representatives will be grateful for the chance to talk. You can hear how their ministries receive, use, and offer what they have, and then make an informed decision on how your congregation's gifts are offered to them.

Use the Bible study on pages 92-97 to examine why you have what you have.

Gifts to regional, national, or global ministries of your larger church can allow the congregation to do God's work beyond the congregation. Inviting representatives of these ministries to speak with you is a good way to honor what they are doing and gives you an opportunity to hear another answer to the question, why do we have what we have?

Summary

- Pleasing most people most of the time is not the leader's goal. Real joy is discovered in gaining knowledge of God and acting accordingly by receiving, using, and offering God's gifts as leading stewards.
- Leaders are needed to rally people around a shared cause and to do the work of management.
- Cultivate leadership and seek representation from the groups in your congregation.
- Leaders recognize the dynamics of change and work within them.
- Leaders are people who propose reasons for why we have what we have.

Chapter 4

Church Asset Management

Christian stewards receive, use, and offer God's gifts,
according to the heart and mind of God.

Building and grounds

Stewards of the church building and grounds see God's abundance in beautiful, welcoming, hospitable places for worship, learning, and service. When this happens, members of the congregation see that the motivation behind well-maintained property goes beyond good care.

It may be useful to talk with new members of a property, building, grounds, or facilities team about the people who have carried on this ministry in the past. Recognizing the faithful stewardship that has gone into making your facilities what they are today may help new members appreciate their work. Your church is a place dedicated to the worship of God. It may have been designed and built for that purpose. A history of time, thought, faith, and effort is part of the story of the congregation.

The stewardship of building and grounds requires a team that ensures good use of resources. Many people take for granted what this team does. There is more to this work than waxing the floors, mowing the lawn, and keeping the roof intact. There are larger expectations. The faithful offering of building and grounds is visible when visitors have the sense that the property is as open to them as to anyone else, because of what is done here, and to whose name it bears witness. Then the property team can see purpose and joy in their work.

Why do we have the property we have?

The answers to that question will help you focus on what is most important. It may make for a good meeting to discuss what is most important about the stewardship ministry of the property team. What would a newcomer to the congregation conclude after the first visit? Is beautification the first consideration? Is maintenance primary?

For some people, the church is the building and is the congregation's first responsibility. For others, the building can always wait.

The stewards who lead the property team can suggest that we have what we have for specific reasons. Does the congregation own its buildings in the same way as the country club owns its buildings? If so, then it is clearly is *our* church and exists for our use, as we see fit. The title to the country-club building gives its owners all rights to the building. The congregation may hold title to a building or buildings, too. Does a title give ownership to the congregation?

God is the owner and we are stewards.

God owns the building and grounds. God is the owner and we are stewards who care for the property on the master's behalf, according to the master's wishes.

What does God want from us, stewards of the church building or buildings and property?

Maintenance is ministry

For a building to meet people's needs for worship, learning, and service, without distraction, it must be well-maintained and have reliable systems. For the property team, maintenance of heating, air conditioning, plumbing, roof surfaces and gutters, security systems, and grounds is part of stewardship ministry.

Preventive maintenance is an investment that can save money. Deferred maintenance is false saving, even when done for good reasons. Many expenses are highly predictable, like clearing fall leaves from the gutters, maintaining roof surfaces, and replacing furnaces and water heaters. With accurate information on purchase dates, warranties, service life, and costs, your team can estimate future expenses related to building maintenance.

The issue of balancing stewardship and property was forced on one congregation, where the global-mission effort became so valued that it came to dominate every aspect of Christian life.

Leaders of the congregation emphasized that money saved at home could be used abroad, and one way to save money was to defer maintenance to the church.

One day, however, a masonry expert took a close look at the building. He knew that he was dealing with people of strong conviction, so he put it to them this way, "If you don't spend some money on the steeple of your church this year, it's going to fall down."

Without a plan, all such expenses may be seen to be unusual and may require a special appeal for funds, or use up already tight current funds, or simply be deferred. A plan allows for a budget.

It may be helpful to look at what percentage of the congregation's budget is spent on maintaining the building and grounds each year. This research could result in a planning calendar that tracks recurring tasks and expenses.

See the "Property Checklist" on pages 98-99.

Compliance with codes

Be aware of municipal ordinances that cover zoning regulations and building codes. Zoning laws establish lawful use for property and may regulate such things as building height, parking requirements, and signage. Building codes are designed to protect people from fires and other safety hazards. Consult public authorities and an attorney if you are considering a change in use of the property (such as turning the church basement into a homeless shelter or day-care center), added use (such as building a parking lot next door), or a building addition.

Safety

Keep your building and grounds as safe as possible. Inspect the property regularly and establish good safety habits such as:

- Sidewalks and driveways are cleared and sanded or salted after snowstorms.

- Snow and ice accumulations on roofs are cleared so that entries are protected from falling snow or ice.
- Handrails and good lighting are installed on stairs and steps.
- Glass doors are marked so people will notice them.
- Floors are free of obstacles or conditions that might cause people to trip or slip.
- Low ceilings and changes in floor level have warning signs.
- Dangerous conditions, such as abandoned buildings or well shafts, are eliminated or made to comply with local regulations.
- Work projects, fund-raising events, and special programs are monitored for unusual hazards, such as use of ladders and lit candles.
- High standards for sanitation are maintained in the kitchen and the congregation complies with any state or local regulations applying to food service or the sale of food.
- Steps have been taken to deal with any asbestos or lead-based paint on the premises.

Equipment

Good stewardship of equipment means regular maintenance.

Record-keeping, accounting, photocopying, and postal demands have predictable annual costs. Start a list with these two categories: 1) critical and vital, and 2) important but not vital. Then work with the staff to prioritize each piece of equipment. The first item listed under the "critical and vital" column might be the church's computer system. If it fails and is unavailable for several days, vital work will not be done, important expectations will not be met, and the staff will feel all the normal pressures grow into potential crises.

Maintenance

Good stewardship of equipment means regular maintenance. Some congregations have staff members who are highly skilled and can meet most service and support needs for computers and other office equipment. The advantage to this situation is that help is available when needed. The disadvantages are that staff members can come and go, and technologies change rapidly.

Local computer companies are finding niche markets in congregations and other organizations. These companies can provide a purchase and maintenance schedule for your individual computers and printers, your network, and related upgrade costs on each piece of equipment so that a real budget can be proposed each year.

Some congregations hide their equipment costs by dramatically deferred maintenance. The initial cost for a computer, software, printer, or network is relatively large. If the equipment seems to work year after year, virtually nothing may be spent after the initial purchase. Then, when a piece of equipment malfunctions in the course of its normal life span, replacement may be the only option.

A data backup strategy is critical. Backup of important data and documents needs to be done twice, so that there is a copy readily available on site and one stored safely off site in the event of fire or flood. Also consider your risk of exposure to computer viruses that can destroy valuable records. Software programs with automatic backup and virus protection are readily available and relatively inexpensive.

Managing risks

A professional risk assessment is a valuable form of protection. Risk-assessment consultants can provide a systematic evaluation of legal exposure in the areas of building accessibility, personnel, and malpractice by lay and ordained staff.

Insurance

Periodically, your congregation should work with your insurance company to research the risks facing your congregation. After this work is done, reports are received, premiums are paid, the value of the property is duly updated, and the leadership may feel secure because of a long-standing relationship with a well-trusted company. But this may not be enough.

See the "Liability Insurance Checklist" on pages 100-101.

As you assess your congregation's insurance coverage and records, research questions such as these:

- Do we know where the congregation's insurance policies are stored?
- What hazards are we protected from in addition to fire and general liability?
- Does the general liability coverage include personal injury?
- In addition to what might be expected, are any other hazards specified?
- Are there umbrella provisions?
- Does our policy provide for full or partial replacement costs?
- Does the replacement value consider new code requirements for such things as accessibility?
- How does depreciation affect replacement costs?
- Do we have an inventory of everything that is in the church?
- Do we have coverage in the event of theft?
- Are volunteers covered at church and at church events?
- Do we have non-owned auto coverage to protect employees and volunteers while driving their own vehicles on congregation business?
- Are our clergy and other counselors covered for misconduct or malpractice?

Evaluating insurance coverage

For each type of coverage purchased by the congregation, ask questions such as these:

- Who is covered?
- How much coverage do you have?
- How is defense of suits funded? What costs would the congregation incur?
- Are all of the activities of the congregation covered, including child care centers, schools, counseling centers, camps, shelters, soup kitchens, recreational programs, and so forth?
- Is coverage limited to events that occur on the premises?

Management of financial assets

Church accounting is similar but not identical to corporate accounting.

Members of a management or finance team are stewards who work to ensure that individual and congregational gifts are faithfully received, used, and offered. Stewards of financial assets uphold the highest standards of organizational accountability, asset management, and reporting. They make an effort to see what the congregational assets are, beyond their place in the accounting system.

Money and power

A new board was meeting for the first time with three new members. People were getting to know each other and learned that one person was the treasurer of a large corporation. It came to everyone's mind at the same time, but only one person spoke to say to him, "I hope that you will consider that job with this board, too." The treasurer's response was revealing: "I'd like to ride along for a while before I drive."

This man understood the treasurer's role to be an important leadership role. He assumed that the church treasurer held the same authority that he appropriately held in a for-profit corporation. The treasurer had yes-no authority, which was respected. All questions were answered with reasons backed up with numbers. What was possible and what was not possible was a matter for the treasurer to decide by basing the decision on sound, for-profit business practices.

Church accounting is similar but not identical to corporate accounting. Each is stewardship in its own way. Each has unique features, especially in how money is viewed and utilized. What counts as an expense is one example of the differences in language and outlook. Is every line item that represents money going out of the treasury an expense? In a for-profit business, the answer is yes. There are many different kinds of expenses, bills, and financial obligations, but money out is simply money out, represented by a minus sign. In a congregation money is connected with deep feelings and faith. Some is meant for what all would agree are expenses: lights, heat, air-conditioning, and so forth. Some is meant to go out of the treasury as a gift, which is not appropriately listed as an expense or obligation.

Offering-plate dollars are gifts from stewards. These dollars are different from business profits or interest income, even though they may be accounted for in similar ways.

The giver's relationship to the congregation is different than the customer's relationship with the company. Expectations are different, and what counts as success is different. The giving of money in worship is not a consumer action. In a congregation, the giving of money is more than paying for expenses or services. It involves faithful receiving, using, and offering according to the mind and heart of God.

Records and reports

Living within the budget can become an end in itself. When this happens the budget guides all considerations, actions, and planning, at all times. These are not reasons to have a budget.

Good records are required and expected. Keeping control of expenses is good stewardship. People expect it. The budget gives evidence of gifts received, used, and offered faithfully and well, in accordance with what the congregation has determined to be God's purposes. Transparent accounting in the congregation gives people confidence that their gifts are well used, not wasted, and can be declared at tax time with accuracy.

Unscrupulous non-profit organizations may speak persuasively of stewardship and mission in much the same way as the congregation does. These organizations attract gifts that may or may not be used as advertised. Part of the congregation's work, however, is to protect its givers. The availability of the balance sheet may not be enough. What measures are in place to ensure transparent accounting? Why is confidence warranted?

Consider doing more than has been required or expected. Good records are required and expected. A separate mid-year financial report may be useful in increasing awareness of the congregation's stewardship of gifts and maintaining and building the confidence of your givers. This report, distributed to every member, also could include a list of projects, accomplishments, and estimates of the number of people who have participated in the congregation's ministries and the number of hours given, to date. What new measures will your congregation put in place?

Receipting and Reporting Standards

The Internal Revenue Service regulations governing non-profit organizations are substantial and change periodically. The most important regulations for congregations are those that classify gifts and specify reporting obligations. Protect your congregation and your givers by contacting a tax attorney or the IRS for the latest information.

See the "Financial Assets Checklist" on pages 102-103.

Handling money

Here are some suggestions for minimizing the risk of negligence and theft, and protecting the members of your congregation:

- Count offering dollars immediately after worship. Many congregations use a system in which two unrelated people who do not handle the congregation's accounting or write checks for the congregation take on this responsibility. The money should not be left alone with either counter at any time. Offering counters total the money and prepare a deposit slip.

- Arrange for the offering to be deposited at the bank.

- Rotate offering counters on a regular basis.

- Do not store cash in the church building.

- Have checks signed by two authorized people and record the check numbers on the invoice or supporting document.

- Form an audit committee and conduct an annual audit. Members of the committee should have training in accounting procedures, if possible, and should use specific procedures recommended by accountants or a qualified outside source.

- Purchase a fidelity bond to cover any fraud or dishonesty by employees or volunteers handling the congregation's funds. A fidelity bond is an insurance policy that protects the congregation against loss of funds through embezzlement or dishonesty.

Donor intent

One of the obligations of receiving gifts is using them as designated.

One of the obligations of receiving gifts is using them as designated. This is a matter of ethics and accounting. If the congregation elects to receive a gift, it is bound by the wishes of the giver. In the sidebar at the bottom of this page, at least the treasurer in the example is honest. There was no pretense. Money is to be used where needed, as may be decided by the leadership and the budget. That may be true in a for-profit business, but money given in a congregation is given according to what the steward believes is God's purposes.

Consider the consequences of a congregation receiving a designated gift only to use it as though there were no intention behind it. Suspicion can be one result. If there are irregularities in this area, are there others? Loss of trust in the leadership and loss of future gifts also may result.

One way to build confidence that donor intent is honored is to have your congregation council or governing board pass a resolution each year establishing a policy that all gifts received by the congregation will be used only for the purposes designated. When this is widely publicized and communicated successfully, people will know that a general fund shortfall will never be made up with funds given for

---

A man came to his church to give a gift, an "over and above gift" designated for a specific purpose that was represented in the church budget.

When he spoke with the treasurer, he expected a short conversation and a "thank you" before he left. What he heard instead was, "No. If you give money that way, it will not be used as designated. It will be used in the general fund as needed. Nothing more than what was budgeted will be given to the cause you have named."

The financial gift eventually was given to the cause he had designated, but not at that church.

another purpose. What measures does your congregation have in place to ensure that donor intent is honored?

Fund-raising

Money from fund-raising activities must be used only for the purposes that have been told to the donors. No matter how much money is raised, the funds cannot be diverted to another purpose without the consent of the donors.

Separation of funds

Restricted funds should be kept in separate accounts from the congregation's operating funds. Restricted funds include funds designated as memorial gifts with interest only to be used, as well as funds intended for limited purposes.

The role of leaders

Taking care of the building, grounds, and equipment may not be seen as part of stewardship ministry in a congregation or these issues may become so pressing that they leave no time for anything else. Then it becomes important for leaders to ask, "Why do we have what we have?" This question can refocus priorities in your building and grounds, property, or management team.

Members of the finance team have more to do than maintain accounting standards.

Handling church finance may seem to involve a straightforward and mundane set of tasks. When it is not seen as a ministry it is nothing more than accounting, nothing more than management and reporting. When that is the case, congregational leaders have stewardship work to do.

Members of the finance team have more to do than maintain accounting standards. They are stewards of others' stewardship, and stewards of the congregation's stewardship. Offered money was given in faith, at worship, for purposes understood to be in line with the heart and mind of Jesus. It is for financial stewards to respect the faithful intent behind gifts given by individuals and the congregation.

Summary

- By taking care of the building, grounds, and equipment and managing risks, the property and management teams provide stewardship ministries in the congregation. These ministries are first and last a witness to the grace of God.

- If money is money only, upholding conventional accounting standards is all that is necessary. If money offered is the gift of the steward, then it is an asset given in faith, to be received in faith, used well, and offered well, according to the heart and mind of God. This is the stewardship ministry of the finance or management team.

Chapter 5

Building Faith,
Increasing Support

Gifts and assets are received well when we are overwhelmed
with the need to give thanks to God.

Your congregation needs to be able to state what gifts and assets it has, what it is doing with them, and why its ministries matter. This work is a stewardship task often carried out in an annual stewardship program. Stewardship programs should be designed to help people live what they believe with the resources that they have.

Paying stewards and giving stewards

Although individual behavior may vary from one situation to the next, in general people see stewardship and stewardship programs in one of two ways.

First, some Christians are *paying stewards*. These people see stewardship in the congregation primarily as a management matter, similar to the work of managing a business or a household. To these people, good stewardship means not wasting money, time, and effort; paying bills on time; and keeping expenses down. For paying stewards, the faithful use of gifts is generally the primary goal. An increase in giving is justified when there are increased expenses, budget shortfalls, or emergencies.

Some Christians, on the other hand, are *giving stewards*. These people also see that good management is good stewardship. They see stewardship in the congregation primarily as a leadership matter, and use stewardship to accomplish long-term strategic goals. An increase in giving is justified when a new vision of ministry identifies needs for new directions, programs, facilities, or staff. Giving stewards and paying stewards need each other and need to understand each other.

Planning a stewardship program

Stewardship programs are planned ministries, led by Christian stewards, with these components:

- giving thanks to God
- communicating your congregation's ministries
- using the assets God has given you to accomplish God's work
- offering to others what God has given to you as a way to accomplish God's work

When these emphases are primary, giving stewards and paying stewards can see that they and the congregation are acting as faithful stewards. Take the following steps to plan a stewardship program for your congregation:

- develop a program budget
- form a "thanking team"
- explore why you have what you have
- educate
- interpret
- ask
- receive

Develop a program budget

A line-item budget provides an answer to this question: How much will we spend to keep the lights and heat on this year? The answer is listed as a dollar amount in the budget. The line-item budget is an important management tool in accounting for income and expenses.

A program budget provides an answer to this question: "Why will we keep the lights on, and why will the heat be turned up this year?"

The answer is a statement of priorities. The program budget is an important leadership tool. It is based on estimates, so it is not accurate as an accounting tool.

When the program budget fits with your congregation's mission statement and strategic plan, you have a powerful leadership and communication tool. A program budget communicates not only what the congregation is doing but also why it matters and how important work is supported.

Most people do not know about most of their congregation's ministries and programs. Even long-time members may be unaware of important ministries. Start constructing a program budget by assembling a representative group from the congregation, giving them paper and markers, and asking them to write down all of the congregation's ministries known to them.

Then look at the total amount, excluding debt reduction, that is needed for operations and to do the congregation's ministries. For example, if the bottom line is $250,000 and 5 percent is the gift for local service ministries, plug in $12,500 alongside a list of the causes those dollars supports, and the amount of the gift given to each.

The congregation's ministry can be extended to people and places it otherwise would never reach by supporting your denomination and its national and global ministries. If 15 percent is given for denominational support in our example, $37,500 would be written down next to an explanation of how those dollars are used.

That leaves $200,000 to place in the proper categories. Many congregations have found that five categories work well to describe their mission: worship, learning, witness, service, and nurturing/fellowship. Make reasonable estimates for all of the categories that are appropriate to your congregation. How much time is spent by the staff and pastor(s) on worship? Have each person estimate the time they spend on this category, and divide each total salary accordingly. Include all related expenses, such as bulletins, lights, heat, and air conditioning. Follow the same procedure for the rest of the categories.

For more on developing a mission statement, see *Our Mission: Discovering God's Call to Us.*

See the "Sample Program Budget" on pages 104-107.

Program budgets are always custom-made. Some congregations will show a higher percentage of dollars for youth ministry than others, because that is what they emphasize and do well. Others may emphasize worship, witness, learning, or nurture.

The program budget is ready when people can take a brief look and say, "Yes, this is our church. This is who we are and what we are doing." At that point, you have a powerful communication and leadership tool that shows how your congregation is distinctive from others in your area.

Form a "thanking team"

Year-round thanksgiving builds faith.

Beginning a stewardship program with planned thanksgiving is an important way to build faith. Form a thanking team to design and implement a year-round thanking program. These people may or may not be part of the stewardship team. Their task is to design and implement a year-round thanking program.

Year-round thanksgiving builds faith. There is room for imagination in who does this and how it is done. What we have, God has given us. Expressions of thanks can come from a variety of people in the form of prayers, themes at worship services, temple talks, letters, Sunday-school programs, and so forth.

For paying stewards, the topic of money in church is about bills and expenses only, not about faithful living. Many of these people feel manipulated when they hear talk of bills and expenses mixed in with talk of God.

For paying stewards, a thanking ministry may create useful confusion. No one expects to get a handwritten thank-you note for paying a bill on time! In most cases, we simply expect a receipt.

Many congregations acknowledge gifts with receipts, which reinforces the notion that money in church is for bills only. Acknowledging gifts with thank-you notes, however, is an important part of a year-round stewardship ministry.

What do you have? What does your congregation have? When we begin to realize what God has given, the experience of abundance can be exceptionally meaningful, even life-changing. The need to give thanks to God can be overwhelming in Christian life.

Explore why you have what you have

Developing a program budget and forming a thanking team are leadership and communication efforts, designed to engage faith. This third step is also meant to engage faith, this time by asking questions that are appropriate for individuals and the congregation:

- Why do we have what we have?
- Why do we have the gifts of the Spirit in such abundance in our congregation?

More specific questions can suggest ministries appropriate for your members and your congregation:

- Why do we have these members with their skills and their willingness to use and offer their gifts?
- Why do we have this building, in this location?
- What do you have? Why do you have it?

Educate

The next step in planning a stewardship program is education. Use presentations, brochures, posters, bulletin inserts, newsletter articles, adult forums, and so forth to provide a complete picture of what the congregation is doing. Highlight your congregation's distinctiveness, what your church has, what it does, and what it plans to do.

At a child's birthday party, all a loving parent wants is a hug or a "thank you." If the child offered the parents a receipt instead, it would hurt because the gift was given as an expression of love.

Interpret

Some people may feel that education is enough, and that if people know what the congregation is doing they will support it—and increase their support each year. This assumption leaves out the remaining steps in a stewardship program. Education answers the *what* of the congregation's work, while interpretation gives answers to the *why*. Once we show what the congregation is doing, we also need to show why these ministries are important, and why they are important to members of the congregation.

A new member might ask, "Why do you have such a large youth ministry?" Your answer can point to God's abundance: "The largest single segment of our membership is under age 18, and the next largest segment is parents of young children. Our children are gifts from God, to be well cared for, and brought up in the faith. That's why the congregation uses so many of our gifts for youth ministry."

Then, your visitor might ask, "Why have you put so much effort into finding out about the community around you? This congregation is surprisingly knowledgeable. It has an impressive understanding of the community around it." Your answer can show how gifts lead to ministries: "To us this is more than information. We see the community around us as our mission field. So we studied and acted on what we learned. Since we know the standard of living, the average age, the average income, and education levels of people in this community, we understand our context, and have found appropriate ways to do ministry. Now we see reasons why we are here, in this neighborhood, and we see how best to use our gifts and assets."

For more on learning about your community, see *Our Context: Exploring Our Congregation and Community.*

Ask

Asking for support is a normal and even essential part of congregational life. As James Hudnut-Beumler point out in *Generous Saints* (Alban Institute, 1999), "A stewardship of money will often flow from a stewardship of time, provided two conditions are met. First the gifts of time must be meaningful, connecting the individual or family members to the religious work that they need to do at the time. . . . Second, the church has to ask for the money" (page 60).

We are God's stewards. Jesus calls people not only to be disciples who follow but to be stewards who serve. God's purposes can be accomplished in our congregation, town or city, nation, and world with the abundance at hand.

Instead of hoarding our assets, we are to use these gifts to fulfill God's purposes. Those who have food are responsible for those who don't. Those who have the good news are responsible to share it where it has not been heard.

We may not realize that asking for something is not "begging," it is not a necessary evil, and it is not something that shouldn't be done in church. Rather, it is part of a steward's ministry, something done by people of faith. In the book *Growing Giver's Hearts* (San Francisco: Jossey-Bass, 2000), Thomas H. Jeavons and Rebekah Burch Basinger point out that for the apostle Paul, asking was a matter of ministry and faith:

> "[Paul] clearly sought to make his fund-raising efforts an extension of his ministry in terms of using his appeals as occasions to teach and preach about the Gospel. He sought to engage motivations for giving in donors that would express and lead to their further growth in faith" (p. 54).

Asking may open up leaders to criticism and objections. But asking and being asked can lead to growth in faith and open up new ways for gifts and assets to be used and offered faithfully.

Asking for support is a normal and even essential part of congregational life.

Receive

For some people, giving at church is a profound part of worship. Some people wish to pledge with envelopes, some expect electronic funds transfer. For others, the church is the best place to give an estate gift. Establish a number of different ways for people to give, through the offering plate, major gifts, end of the year gifts, and electronic funds transfer.

Some do, some don't give: Every congregation has a large segment of non-givers. If your congregation receives one-half or more of its gifts from 20 to 25 percent of the members, you are in the same situation as most churches in the United States. Leaders may be tempted to see this large group of non-givers as an opportunity. It's easy to think that if this group started paying, everyone's share could go down or if this group started giving, ministries could expand. Many of these people may attend worship fairly regularly. They may be active members and appear to have the ability to support the church financially. But in fact they don't. Most of these people will not become regular givers. They may give for an emergency or at Christmastime, but not regularly or in any predictable way. Stewardship programs will not reach them. Because of this, don't expect regular increases from people in this group, or expect that many of them will become regular givers.

Expect the majority of increases to come from your current givers.

Current givers are those who pledge, as well as those who give regularly but do not pledge. These people often are current and former officers, leaders, volunteers, and long-time members. They can talk from the heart about their personal stake in the health of the con-gregation.

Among current givers, there may be an agreed-upon, hidden status quo about how much is expected from everyone from year to year. There may be united resistance when an increase larger than expected is asked for, especially if there is no emergency. Nonetheless, expect the majority of increases to come from your current givers.

Potential givers: Some members will have an experience of God's abundance through your stewardship program. For them, a new world will open up. This can happen when individuals and congregations reflect on these questions:

- What do we have?
- Why do we have it?
- How have we received it?
- How will we use what we have well?
- How will we give what we have well?

Potential givers are those who become new leaders or team members in the congregation. New tasks may reveal new gifts they didn't recognize earlier. Over time, they may be able to speak from their heart about how much the congregation has come to mean to them.

Summary

A stewardship program works to engage faith, raise up the congregation's ministries, and form stewards. It will include plans to:

- give thanks to God
- communicate your congregation's ministries
- use the assets God has given to accomplish God's work
- offer to others what God has given us to as a way to accomplish God's work

Follow these steps to plan a stewardship program:

- develop a program budget
- form a "thanking team"
- explore why you have what you have
- educate
- interpret
- ask
- receive

Chapter 6

Last Year Didn't Go Well

*Stewardship programs are ministries of the church. They are
first and last a witness to the grace of God.*

Ministry teams leading a congregation's financial stewardship
program work to display God's abundance to individuals and to the
congregation. Starting from this point, all God's gifts and blessings
may be thankfully received, faithfully used, and generously offered by
individuals and the congregation. This chapter lays out several types
of comments or reactions to a financial stewardship program and
reasons why the program may not have met the desired goals.

We didn't do a program this year

*"We pushed hard last year. Our people need a rest. We don't want to
be seen as only about money. But we received a much smaller
increase than last year."*

Did we assume that the increase seen last year would simply be
repeated, even without a stewardship program? Did we assume that
any increase is so unusual that it could not happen two years in a row?

Some people will feel nothing but "money pressure," no matter
how gracious the stewardship program is. If the resulting increase is
substantial or unusual, some will conclude that the only way such an
increase could have been accomplished was with a hard-edged push,
which cannot be repeated successfully every year. If the budget and
cash flow are the only truly urgent matters for a stewardship program
or a congregation, people will understandably get tired of hearing
about budgets and cash flow.

Some people are unable to imagine how anything above expenses could be used well by the congregation. For these members, explain not only how the congregation receives and uses gifts faithfully, but also how its gifts are offered faithfully.

You may wish to say . . .

- "God will be generous with us again this year. We will see reasons for gratitude again this year."
- "Our members expect to use and to offer what they have received from God."
- "We will do our best to assist with ministries that lift up God's generosity."
- "No congregation is only about money."
- "Stewardship of financial resources is part of congregational life."

Actions to consider

Involve many people in your stewardship program. Do what you do best and stick closely to God's grace and gospel.

Did we outrun our support?

"We tried. We had a good program. Everyone seemed supportive. No one suggested that we were on the wrong track. The appeal failed and the goal was not reached, but no one has suggested that we were at fault in any way. No one has suggested that we failed. We are hearing some of the usual objections again, but for the most part life goes on as before."

How important was the goal? Was it crucial that the program succeed? Was the increase proposed for normal budget matters only? If so, it may have caught the interest only of those few people who understand and care deeply about the church's budget, and no one else. Under these circumstances, expect about what was received last year.

Behind the comments

After a year like this, the stewardship committee may need to listen to some objections, such as "We're already giving as much as we can," "We'll need more commitment," and "We'll need more members before the budget can go up that much." These are instructive comments. They have the desired effect of getting the congregation off the hook and getting the stewardship team off the hook, so that no one is to blame. Some new to the team may find this puzzling. Is it okay to fail? It may be that the leaders of the congregation, and the 20 percent of the members who give the most, did not see a compelling reason to raise their giving.

You may wish to say . . .

We will continue to say the stewardship message of God's gracious giving.

- "We are sorry that we failed you this year. We will work hard again next year. We will continue to say the stewardship message of God's gracious giving. We are all aware that there are overwhelming reasons for gratitude to God, and we will continue to raise them up this year."
- "Next year we anticipate no truly pressing budget needs, but our ministry goals may be higher than ever before."

Actions to consider

Ask a stewardship question, such as these: "Why do we have what we have? What is God calling us to do with what we have been entrusted with?" The answer may ignite your congregation. Then, find the leadership, ask for support, and be open to growing in faith as a result.

Our program was a gospel ministry

"We know that the team is responsible for more than the budget. Yes, budget matters are important, but the budget is not as urgent as matters of faith. So our program emphasized the gospel. We said

it all well: God gives gifts that we receive thankfully, use well, and offer faithfully. We received about what we received last year. But the objections we heard afterward all suggested that we over-emphasized money! What's going on?"

How new was the gospel emphasis? The gospel may have been an unexpected part of the stewardship program.

Behind the comments

For some people, a stewardship program is about needs and budgets but has nothing to do with faith. Sheer force of habit may have prevailed. Year after year, some people have seen stewardship programs that were concerned only with financial pressure. So that is what they learn to hear. Others may object as a matter of habit. Some people will be startled and changed by gracious stewardship talk. Some will not.

You may wish to say . . .

- "The stewardship team voted recently to make some changes. The changes have already begun. This is what we did. We asked several of our members to increase their giving by one-third, even though our budget is secure for the year. We suggested that this is a way to live joyfully with what we have, and it seems to be a faithful way to use and offer what we have been entrusted with. Everyone we asked said yes."
- "By the end of the year we hope that our congregation will be able to offer more support to more of the ministries we care about. You are welcome to do the same."

Actions to consider

The team's first task may be to break the traditional expectations of what a stewardship program is and does. Trust in God's promises means that the gospel will prevail. Stay positive! Old habits do not disappear quickly. The work next year may not be substantially different than this year. The goal again will be to emphasize what is most pressing for Christian people: giving thanks to God, receiving well, using well, offering faithfully what God has given us, and growing in faith.

There's not enough commitment

"We know how to talk to our people. There has long been an agreement on the stewardship team to emphasize commitment, year-long giving, and pledging, as we have done with good success in the past. The fact that it didn't seem to work last year must mean that we did not find enough committed people, or enough commitment in our members. Or it could be that values have changed, that young people don't have as much commitment as before."

Did the same people lead the stewardship program this year as the year before? Is our committee made up of one age group? Do we expect younger people to live as stewards the same way as older people? Do we expect younger people to give, even if they are not represented in leadership, or are not heard when they are in leadership? Did we look for substantial increases from a large group of non-givers?

Behind the comments

There may be some hesitancy to adopt something new in place of what worked before. There may be no apparent reasons to change and current supporters may suggest that it seems risky to change.

You may wish to say . . .

- "It may be that we are communicating as effectively as before."
- "It may also be that our most effective communication speaks to only one segment of the congregation. If so, a large number of people did not hear what we thought we were saying to everyone."

Actions to consider

Provide multiple giving opportunities. If one group wants to express their faith as commitment, with long-term giving, it is important to know that. For some, this is the way stewardship is done. These people may also be happy to give to an institution, for institutional support. Another group of givers may see the congregation as a place for community and compassion. They may favor short-term giving opportunities. Their preference may be to give to a program or cause or special appeal. They are happy to give to the youth program, or to children's education, as these programs require support during the year.

Ask people from different generations to serve on the team coordinating the stewardship program. Ask them how they live their Christian lives. What speaks well to one generation may not communicate at all to another.

One way to be sensitive to generational differences is to provide more than one way for members to offer their gifts of time, expertise, standing, and money. What has worked in the past might be working with only one generation now. Does your congregation offer members wide opportunities for participating in its mission and ministry? How do these opportunities enrich the faith of your members?

Provide multiple giving opportunities.

All we need is more . . .

"If our attendance was better, we would be better off. If we had more members, or higher attendance, or more people pledging, our budget would be better."

Oddly enough, some congregations do not actually want more, because they are fairly comfortable with what they have and who they are. This is hard to notice at first because there may be serious talk of the wish for more givers or more generosity. New givers are welcome, but only in order to make up the nagging monthly shortfalls in the budget, and only as long as the new givers do not suggest change, disturb tradition, or alter the leadership status quo.

Behind the comments

There may be a lack of confidence that giving by the current membership can support the church. Your may hear "Our giving isn't worthwhile. We can't do it."

You may wish to say . . .

Raise sights by appealing to faith.

• "We already have everything we need to do what God wants us to do. There is far more to us than seeing what we don't have."

• "Let's look at what we do have, where we see God's abundance in our congregation."

Actions to consider

Raise sights by suggesting that there are other reasons to explain why we have what we have apart from our contentment. Raise sights by appealing to faith. We can grow in the knowledge of God and receive, use, and offer our gifts faithfully.

We didn't ask

"We worked hard to educate our people. When we were done most people knew that biblical stewardship is a matter at the heart of our Christian faith. Giving at our church is utterly private, an intimate matter between the giver and God."

Some people are certain that their level of giving is correct, and they see giving as a measure of individual faith. These people are puzzled when giving by others does not increase.

Behind the comments

Some people may believe that no one has any real claim on what they have. They believe that what belongs to them is theirs to use as they see fit. These people need to hear about God's choices, God's abundance, God's gifts, and God's wishes.

Here are some positive responses to stewardship programs:

- Thanks for putting thanks to God first.

- Thanks for showing us that the most urgent matters in the Christian life are also the most urgent matters in the life of the congregation.

- I felt unusually blessed this year! What kind of stewardship program does that?

- I see more opportunities to serve than I did before.

- I'm beginning to see how much I can do, and how much our congregation can do.

- I am beginning to see why I have what I have.

Giving in a congregation is more than a private matter. The gifts of individuals enable the congregation to act as a steward, using gifts in ministries within and outside the congregation.

Everything we have belongs to God.

You may wish to say . . .

- "Everything we have belongs to God."
- "As stewards, we are called to receive, use, and offer our gifts in response to God's abundance."

Actions to consider

It may be wise to start small. Will the your ministry team lead by being the first to sign on or pledge? People may ask why you did this, ahead of time. That will be an opportunity for you to say, "We were asked. It was clear that the person asking did so as a matter of faith. We believe that our congregation's assets and gifts are well used in what is proposed for next year."

Learning from objections

All comments and objections are potentially helpful to your team. They can help you to see how members of the congregation understand or do not yet understand the relationship between what they believe and what they have.

Some comments and objections are religious, some are social in nature. Some are meant well and help the team to do better work. Some are done out of habit and are difficult to change. Some comments may arise repeatedly in the life of the congregation to:

- enforce the status quo
- limit the scope of the team's work
- justify the failures of the congregation and the team
- blame the program
- justify personal shortcomings with pious talk
- silence the pastor's witness to the stewardship message

One reason why objections survive is because they can give a ministry team all the room they need to do nothing, even giving them permission to fail, without consequences, and with community support. Failure is often the expected result, especially where money is concerned.

The role of the pastor

How the pastor receives, uses, and offers God's gifts is a public witness.

The pastor is not immune from the power of possessions and money. How the pastor receives, uses, and offers God's gifts is a public witness. How those tasks are accomplished in the life of the pastor can have a significantly positive impact on the congregation's outlook. Pastors can be leaders in stewardship by:

- preaching the texts
- preaching what they practice, if they have discovered joy in giving
- leading by example
- supporting leaders in the congregation

- emphasizing the faithful receiving, use, and offering of gifts as important matters of faith

Summary

- All comments and objections are potentially helpful to your team. They can help you to see how members of the congregation understand or do not yet understand the relationship between what they believe and what they have.

Chapter 7

Commercial and Denominational Materials

Commercial and denominational stewardship materials that have an emphasis on the gospel, an educational component, and a clear appeal to faith can be gifts to your congregation.

Effective stewardship programs involve organized efforts of teaching, leading by example, and stating expectations. Materials and kits produced commercially or by your denomination can offer fresh approaches and can be worth all the effort when well led. These programs are complete when they say the gospel and include an education component, a communication component, a clear appeal to faith, a clear appeal for support, and a strategy for thanking or acknowledgement.

Your expectations

The most important part of any stewardship program may be your expectations. What do you want to accomplish with the program? Do you see your work as a ministry, and wish to do the work of teaching about the Bible and helping your members grow in faith? Do you wish to open up ways to live the faith in how your congregation receives, uses, and offers its gifts?

Do you have high or low expectations for the program? Do you air your doubts or do you air your confidence in what your congregation can accomplish? Positive leadership can make up for weak programs, while negative leadership can hinder the success of the best programs.

Are you looking for the "right" program for your church and your circumstances that will please everyone, generate enthusiasm throughout all the congregation, and solve all giving problems? Are you looking for a program that will turn irregular givers into loyal pledgers, or activate inactive givers? This kind of ideal program does not exist.

Give the program a chance

The authors of commercial and denominational stewardship materials may not know your congregation at all, but they may be very acquainted with the characteristics of churches of the same size. These characteristics may be more applicable to your circumstances than you might guess. The promised results may be realistic. There may be good reasons for optimism if stewardship materials come with a proven record of success.

Stewardship materials or kits usually are the result of experience and knowledge, tested by practice. In all probability unworkable elements have been eliminated from the materials. What appears unwieldy or overdone may in fact be exactly right, proven by experience. It may be unwise to make changes and expect the advertised results.

The role of leaders

Leaders serve the congregation well when they are personally enthusiastic. Members are more likely to gain confidence from what they see in their leaders than from what they see in the program. The chances of success increase when leaders are willing to lead by example. When leaders are prepared to meet objections, people's minds can be changed about the value of the program.

The pastor is one leader among many needed for success.

The pastor is one leader among many needed for success. The pastor can make the point that stewardship programs are essential ministries for Christian growth by suggesting that they would be necessary every year, even if the budget was raised by 30 percent every year and offerings increased by 35 percent every year. Stewardship programs are necessary in order to receive well, use well, and offer well, work that may or may not be done if the budget is always met or exceeded.

Should the congregation know what the pastor is giving? Yes, as a steward's witness to God's generosity. The pastor or the pastor's family can make the point of stewardship, leading by example. If the pastor can do this as part of an expected witness to faith—not as bragging or shaming—then a public witness to the pastor's giving can be effective in leading to growth in faithful receiving, using, as well as offering.

The value of a third party

If you or your ministry team are planning to lead a stewardship program, you may appreciate the value of another leader at the table, one who is not a member of the congregation. This leader may be a specialist employed by the denomination or judicatory to work with congregations. These specialists often are available at little or no cost.

Their visits can be the occasion for new thinking and new programs of stewardship ministry. They may be able to evaluate particular stewardship programs with you, receive questions that might not be put to the pastor, and be more persuasive to your group because of their objectivity. Call your judicatory office to find out what is available in your area.

A specialist from outside your congregation may be able to say what needs to be said, things the pastor cannot say without jeopardy to relationships, such as these:

- The way out of the funding crisis is to ask your current givers to give more.
- No one's giving is entirely a matter between God and themselves.
- The most vocal critics of stewardship programs are most often those who give the least, and may in fact give nothing.

The large financial gift was almost half of the congregation's annual budget. At first the presence of a large undesignated amount of money caused no trouble. Then, in the summer, there was a budget shortfall.

For the first few months, only the interest was used. Before long, the interest was necessary every month. Not long after that principal was needed and used for two years. When the gift was gone, it wasn't clear to anyone how the congregation would manage.

The congregation knew that the next stewardship program would decide whether or not they would continue as a congregation. To the surprise of many, more than was needed was pledged.

Retaining a consultant

If your congregation chooses to retain a consultant for a stewardship program, capital appeal, debt reduction drive, or major increase in annual giving, consider these important questions:

- Do your congregation's needs match up with services provided?
- Does the leadership style fit with the congregation's other leaders?
- Does the consultant give evidence of a spiritual outlook that reflects your faith and values?
- Is the consultant personally compatible with your congregation?

Summary

To evaluate commercial and denominational stewardship programs, look for the following:

- the gospel message of God's gracious giving
- an education component
- a communication component
- a clear appeal to faith
- a clear appeal for support
- a strategy for thanking/acknowledging members for their support

Chapter 8

Endowment Funds

Congregational endowment funds can benefit individuals, families,
the congregation, and other Christian ministries and agencies.

Providing a way for the congregation to receive large gifts, use these gifts effectively, and offer annual gifts in support of Christian ministries is faithful stewardship. One way to do this is through an endowment fund.

Why do this?

See the "Sample Endowment Policy" on pages 108-110.

A congregational endowment provides important stewardship services to members, the congregation, and ministries and causes that are doing God's work in the world.

A congregational endowment is a perpetual fund. The initial dollars placed in the fund remain in the fund as principal. Interest generated by the principal is distributed annually as decided by the congregation or designated by the donors.

An endowment fund provides members of your congregation the opportunity to see accumulated resources as an asset requiring faithful planning and decision-making. An endowment fund is a way to receive large gifts of cash or property and use them well. A sample endowment policy is included in the tools section of this book.

Do you have members who have named your congregation as a beneficiary in their wills? Is your congregation prepared to receive a large, undesignated amount of money?

The gift can be a blessing when the congregation is prepared to receive and use it well. It can build awareness of God's abundance, lead to growth in awareness of what a congregation can do, and support ministries and Christian agencies that people care deeply about.

A large financial gift can be a curse, however, when the dollars are allowed into the monthly budget. Monthly offerings that sustained the work before the gift now are not enough, even though they were before. Congregational conflict and loss of confidence can result.

Refusing to be dependent on large gifts is one way to maintain financial confidence. In this approach, current giving is used for current ministries. That is, the monthly offering goes for monthly expenses.

The way through conflicts over large gifts is to determine how such gifts are to be used before any gift is received.

Large-gift stewardship

The faithful receiving, use, and offering of estate gifts requires advance planning and consideration of these questions:

- What kind of committee or team is best for this work?
- Who will do the work of investment?
- Who will decide how interest income should be offered?

Faithful reception

It is likely that your congregation will receive an estate gift at some time. Readiness to receive such a gift is a matter of faith, policy, and ethics. Christian stewards may see that the faithful offering of accumulated assets is a natural outcome of a lifetime of giving. Stewardship on their part will be to ensure that the gift is a blessing and not a curse to the congregation or another ministry.

Readiness to receive an estate gift requires a policy that reflects good leadership. If an endowment fund is established, protection of the principal must be guaranteed. Interest only is offered in support of Christian ministries. When a probate lawyer delivers a large check to the congregation, members already know how and where the money will be invested and used. In addition, the congregation has reserved the right to accept or not accept an estate gift. If the gift endows the construction of a new building, with no provisions for maintenance, the congregation may not be in a position to receive the gift and use it as designated.

The ethical matter in receiving an estate gift into an endowment fund is ensuring donor intent. Part of the trust involved in any endowment is the assurance that gifts received will only be used as designated. If that assurance is broken, good stewards will have legitimate reservations about giving an estate gift. If the gift is undesignated, interest is used only as specified in the endowment policy.

Faithful use

If your congregation establishes an endowment fund, who will do the work of investment for your congregation? On the one hand, the team responsible for your endowment fund is obliged to invest with able, trustworthy people. There may be members with investment expertise, for whom the congregation's endowment would be new business. The reputation of these people is not in doubt. They are good members, trustworthy, and fully able. Shouldn't they be on the endowment team? Shouldn't they handle the money for the congregation?

On the other hand, will that member be able to serve a term of office on the team if investment is done solely through him or her? What happens when the stock market drops, or interest rates fall, and the endowment loses money? Should the congregation put a member in such a position?

If the investing is done by a third-party financial advisor outside of the congregation, objectivity is gained, no one member is identified with how the fund performs, and the team can explain that losses, when they occur, are a normal part of investing, no matter who does the work.

What about us?

There are two schools of thought on the question of using endowment interest for congregational needs. One group says that no interest dollars are ever used appropriately for congregational needs or programs. Those programs, whether annual or capital, are best supported and funded by members. This protects annual stewardship because there is no source of income for the congregation's programs other than the gifts of members. When capital is needed for a new building, for example, it is built with gifts from members, who are willing to give to what they care deeply about.

The danger in this course of action is that large, unexpected expenses can only be funded through monthly offerings. The result could be unwelcome cutbacks in important programs, or long-term debts funded solely by the current budget.

Another school of thought suggests that under limited circumstances, interest income from endowment funds may be well used for the capital or maintenance needs of the congregation. This ensures that large, unexpected expenses will not interfere with important current ministries, and maintenance that might otherwise be deferred will happen on time, before it becomes a larger expense.

The danger is that endowing programs takes away the need to give. If ministries we care deeply about are well supported through an endowment, they don't need our money. If people see no need for their gifts of money, it won't be long before they lose interest in contributing altogether. In the end, all that once-vital programs will have left is money, and nothing else.

Another danger is the strong potential for hoarding. If members perceive that the congregation has all the money it will ever need, people may see no need to consider a major gift even when the need for capital is greater than what is available in the endowment. Endowment funds should not be seen as providing the security that comes with protecting the money we will need for any conceivable circumstance.

Faithful offering

How will the interest from an endowment fund be given away, and who will decide? A policy guiding how interest will be disbursed is essential to guide an endowment fund team and ensure the congregation's trust in the process.

Faithful offering by the congregation can be accomplished in several ways. The congregation may establish a policy with categories to be used for all undesignated gifts. Often percentages are used, as in this example:

- A minimum of 20 percent for community outreach, seminaries, colleges, students, social service agencies, and people in our congregation with special needs.
- A minimum of 20 percent for the mission of the church beyond our congregation, including world hunger, people in poverty, new congregations, and so on.
- A minimum of 20 percent for our congregation's capital improvements and debt reduction.
- Up to 40 percent for any one or all of the above designated areas.

The congregation should approve the overall guidelines for distribution. One option is for an endowment team to bring proposals to the congregation council each year. These proposals are then voted on by representatives elected by the congregation. The congregation is under no obligation to disburse income every year.

Another option is for an endowment team to bring proposals to the annual meeting each year. In this case the team presents the categories and percentages to the congregation for a vote. This procedure is effective when the meeting is held at the beginning of the year, before any gifts are received. When undesignated estate gifts are received during the year, there is no further reason to vote, since the matter has been decided beforehand.

The role of leaders

Visionary leaders who raise people's appreciation of what they have and what can be accomplished will offer persuasive reasons to establish an endowment. Leaders who are managers can ensure that the legalities are well covered.

Another role for leaders is to prevent an endowment fund and investment from becoming ends unto themselves. When that happens, the most important part of an endowment is the endowment, not the good stewardship it makes possible, and not the ministries it supports. When a congregation loses its way with an endowment, protecting what is "theirs" starts to take precedence over properly offering what has been entrusted to them. Annual meetings start to look more like shareholder conventions than the body of Christ.

How a congregation receives, uses, and offers money and property reflects its spiritual values.

The pastor's role

One of the pastor's leadership roles is to help discern what God is calling the congregation to do with what it has. The pastor asks in a variety of ways and settings, "Why do we have what we have?"

Another role for the pastor is to do the hard work of pointing to faith and stewardship concerns in matters of money and property. Money and property are always in real or potential conflict with faith in God and can even displace faith. How a congregation receives, uses, and offers money and property reflects its spiritual values, which determine our principles, outlook, behavior, and commitments.

The pastor's leadership by example includes having a will, updating it, and the willingness to state publicly that having a will ensures that the values of his or her faith will guide the disbursement of accumulated assets.

Summary

- Establishing an endowment and receiving endowment gifts can be occasions for long-term growth in faith and outreach.
- Congregations that know why they have what they have work to receive large gifts thankfully, use them faithfully, and offer them generously for the work of God in the world.
- Faithful stewardship of large gifts requires leaders who work to establish a policy and guidelines that are well-known and widely understood by the members in a congregation.

Conclusion

How Far Can We See?

*The thing that Christian stewards want most
is to live where Jesus is the master.*

We have only begun to see God's abundance.

Jesus announced the dawn of the new age, the coming kingdom of God, a new heaven and a new earth, in which the former things have passed away.

God's kingdom reveals to us an invaluable pearl. Where Jesus is the master not one in a hundred is left behind, prodigal sinners are received home as family again, generosity beyond anything previously known is offered to those who worked all or part of the day.

We want to live there.

Glimpses of new light are all around us. The new dawn fully lights up the old world. If we are distressed by what we see, it is because we know the mind of the master. Some people will not eat today. In the new light we can't help but see them, as Jesus sees them. We know Jesus' wishes for hungry people, for people in poverty, for those in all types of need. They may see God's abundance for the first time in what we do.

How far can we see?

The new light gives new perspective on why we have what we have. We can see past scarcity. We can see past our own needs and our desire to indulge ourselves. We can see past the rationalizations that allow inequities to continue, with no effect on our consciences or lifestyles. We can also see that what God most wants us to have, God provides.

Recommended Resources

Books

Cox , W. Michael, and Richard Alm. *Myths of Rich and Poor: Why We're Better off Than We Think*. New York: Basic Books, 1999.

Durall, Michael. *Creating Congregations of Generous People*. Bethesda, Maryland: Alban Institute, 1999.

Grimm, Eugene. *Generous People: How to Encourage Vital Stewardship*. Nashville: Abingdon, 1992.

Hanna, Jeffrey W. *Safe and Secure: The Alban Guide to Protecting Your Congregation*. Bethesda, Maryland: Alban Institute, 1999.

Haynes, Wesley, Andrew Rudin, and J. Thomas Ryan. *Inspecting and Maintaining Religious Properties*. New York: Landmarks Conservancy, 1991.

Hoge, Dean R., ed. *Money Matters: Personal Giving in American Churches*. Louisville: Westminster John Knox Press, 1996.

Hoge, Dean, Patrick McNamara, and Charles Zech. *Plain Talk About Churches and Money*. Bethesda, Maryland: Alban Institute: 1997.

Hudnut-Beumler, James. *Generous Saints*. Bethesda, Maryland: Alban Institute, 1999.

Jeavons, Thomas H., and Rebekah Burch Basinger. *Growing Giver's Hearts*. San Francisco: Jossey-Bass, 2000.

Joiner, Donald W., and Norma Wimberly, eds. *The Abingdon Guide to Funding Ministry: An Innovative Sourcebook for Church Leaders*, vols. 1, 2, and 3. Nashville: Abingdon Press, 1995, 1996, 1997.

Meeks, Douglas M. *God the Economist: The Doctrine of God and Political Economy*. Minneapolis: Fortress Press, 1989.

Rendle, Gilbert. *Leading Change in the Congregation*. Bethesda, Maryland: Alban, 1998.

Reumann, John. *Stewardship and the Economy of God*. Eerdmans Publishing Company, 1992.

Ronsvalle, John, Sylvia Ronsvalle, and U. Milo Kaufmann. *At Ease: Discussing Money and Values in Small Groups*. Bethesda, Maryland: Alban Institute, 1998.

Stanley, Thomas J., and William D. Danko. *The Millionaire Next Door: The Surprising Secrets of America's Wealthy*. Atlanta: Longstreet Press, 1996.

Vallet, Ronald E. *Stepping Stones of the Steward: A Faith Journey Through Jesus' Parables*, 2nd edition. Grand Rapids: Eerdmans Publishing, 1994.

Wheeler, Sondra Ely. *Wealth as Peril and Obligation*. Grand Rapids: Eerdmans, 1995.

Wuthnow, Robert. *The Crisis in the Churches: Spiritual Malaise, Fiscal Woe*. New York: Oxford University Press, 1997.

Reports

Church Law and Tax Report. Matthew, North Carolina: Christian Ministry Resources. Updated annually.

Maintenance Manual: A Program for Inspection and Seasonal Maintenance of Religious Properties. Architecture and Building Commission of the Roman Catholic Diocese of Albany, 1985.

Web sites

- Evangelical Lutheran Church in America (ELCA) Office of the Treasurer: www.elca.org/ot/congregations/conghelp.html

- ELCA Stewardship: www.elca.org/dcm/stewardship

- The Planned Giving Resource Center, The General Board of Discipleship, Nashville: www.gbod.org/stewardship

Chapter 2 Tool

More Than Enough: An Asset-Based Planning Process

A few words

An asset-based approach to planning begins with primarily positive presumptions about the task at hand and the participants' capabilities to engage the task effectively. The following pages outline a simple process by which any planning group can discover their assets for almost any intended outcome and can progress through completion of the task together.

Materials you will need

The planning process requires the following materials and resources:

- Felt-tip markers, at least two per participant
- Medium-sized slips of paper, card stock or poster board, about 25 to 30 per participant
- A large work space, such as several tables pulled together, a large open floor space, or a large, empty wall space
- Tape

The first step, asset listing

Assemble the individuals who will engage in the planning process. They should have some general awareness of the task at hand (for example, "We will be working on our annual picnic") and a general familiarity and trust with each other. Follow these steps:

- To engage in the first step, reacquaint participants with the general task or program or direction they are charged with planning and answer questions about the task.

- Briefly state the process by which participants will plan, and its characteristics:

  A. We will be the planning group, and have sole responsibility for carrying out the plans.

  B. We have everything and everyone we need right here and right now to get done what we want to have happen.

  C. We will work at only what we're good at doing and what we like to do.

  D. We will approach the entire planning process from the viewpoint of possibilities, not problems. We will get done what we plan.

  E. Nothing stands in our way.

- Distribute slips of paper to participants—about 25 to 30 slips to each person—and at least two markers. Explain that in the next 10 to 15 minutes they will list their individual assets, one per piece of paper, that might in any way be helpful to the completion of the assigned task. Each slip of paper should name an asset and include the person's initials or name.

- If they need help in defining *asset*, remind them that an asset is known by its utility or usefulness for a task. A *gift* is known by its giving and receiving, but assets are elements of a person that can be leveraged for a useful purpose. Finally, an asset has a certain tangibility to it, or at least can be easily seen and recognized by others. (So in their writing, participants should be as specific as possible in recording their assets.)

- As participants begin to write their assets on individual slips of paper, remind them of several salient aspects of "asset-based

planning:" An asset can be a personal trait, education or training, or personal experience. It can include a person's skills, specific history, or relationships. Assets includes things, too, like
land and tools. And finally, there are many assets each person
possesses that may have lain dormant for many years (for
example, a musical talent or an unclaimed personal favor).

- Don't let participants come to an end in their writing, but keep
  inserting reminders (above) that characterize other ways to
  think about assets they possess for the work. The object is to
  fill the work space with assets of participants. Keep reminding
  participants that they are writing down what they like to do
  and what they are good at doing. Also remind them that assets
  are always at hand, ready to be used, including even those
  assets that haven't been used in a while. An asset starts to be a
  problem when it does not really exist (for example, I'd like to
  know how to teach teenagers about Jesus) or when it is not
  accompanied by personal passion or high interest (for example, someone should do this, and it might as well be me).

- Redundancy is expected and welcomed in the process. This
  means that, for example, if five people know the same public
  official (as a relational asset), all five of them should include
  that relationship in their assets list.

The second step, asset-mapping

In the second step, participants make sense out of the enormous and perhaps overwhelming amount of assets available for
the work they are about to do. This step is familiar to those participants who have participated in advanced brainstorming activities, or have worked with "mind-maps" in their professions.
Participants will now make a "map" of their assets by performing
a simple clumping of asset slips on the work surface. Participants
can follow these directions:

1. Walk around the table (floor area or wall space) and make sure you understand all the items that have been listed. Ask questions of the group members whose listed assets seem confusing or ambiguous.

2. Write and add new asset slips as you walk around and are reminded of similar assets you possess.

3. When you have finished this exploratory and asset-internalizing activity, begin "clumping together" assets that seem to connect. They may be the same category, have a cause-and-effect relationship, be sub-categories of a larger category, or have the same tone or character to them.

4. Take plenty of time for this kind of mapping, because participants need to internalize the wealth of the assets they possess for the task and start to grapple with the similarities of broad categories. The stronger the clumps (the more slips that appear in that category) the more likely most members of the group possess a similar asset and, later, a similar passion for a task or activity.

During this time, your leadership task is to keep the group moving toward an informal consensus about the mapping results, so that participants have considered the categories and sub-categories, made adjustments, discovered some preliminary patterns, and worked past what is immediately obvious.(In this role you may have to ask questions such as, "Are you sure about the categories?" or "Could you combine—or break apart—some of your categories?" This will help in the deeper thinking process. These programs are complete when they say the gospel and include an education component, a communication component, a clear appeal to faith, a clear appeal for support, and a strategy for thanking or acknowledgement.

The final part of this step is to tape together all the asset slips in each category and, if space permits, tape the whole map together in its relationships, categories taped to other categories. This "freezing" of the map into a semi-permanent state will keep it readily available in the future, when participants are working on further steps in a planning process and may be tempted to forget the wealth of assets available to them, and their inter-relationships.

The third step, summarizing patterns

In this step, you start to collect together the patterns you see in your group's asset map. The step is both simple and profound, and consists of these possible actions:

1. On a separate sheet of paper, collect participants' responses to the question, "What are we—this group of asset-blessed folks here right now—good at, and/or what do we like to do?" (The emphasis is on characterizing the group by its assets.)

2. As you write their answers, do not include any hint of negativity or hesitancy. The point of the summarizing is to condense into one place the sharpest, most positive, most hopeful description of this group's assets.

3. Do not list next steps or tasks yet. That comes soon enough, and can't happen in the spirit of asset-based planning until this summary is done.

4. You may want to circle, star, or otherwise emphasize especially strong patterns of assets within the group, or use arrows to show connectivity among the assets of this group.

The fourth step, looking at next steps

In asset-based ways of thinking, "planning" is "taking the next step." The presumption of this thought process is that the steps evolve, one success at a time. Because individuals are working only at what they enjoy doing and are skilled and experienced at, the steps come more easily, are accomplished more quickly and efficiently, and yield to next steps more quickly. Thus, the time saved from a lengthy planning process is applied to repeated asset listing and mapping, brief decision-making and action. As you take next steps in the planning process, work through these actions:

1. The basic question for the group is simple, "Based on our assets as a group—and the proposition that we will work at what we're good at doing—what are the next steps we can take, who will undertake each step and by when?"

2. Insist that the next steps stay within the general parameters of the task you have originally accepted and that each individual task is assigned to someone who is capable and willing to undertake the task.

3. It is important that individuals suggest and accept individual next steps that match their individual assets, not the group's generalized assets. Because you still have in front of you the map of the individual assets, you can refer to those.

4. If at any time a next step is not accepted or suggested by someone who has that capability, do not list that task. Otherwise, the spirit and power of an asset-based process will again be subsumed into "duty" or "necessity."

5. List the tasks by action, responsible person, and due date. If possible, group tasks by a logic of connectivity, with similar tasks listed close together.

6. When the list seems complete—most assets of the group have been applied and/or the internal requirements of the next step have been met—summarize what you have agreed upon and double check the level of participants' attachment to and interest in the tasks.

The fifth step, elements of a bigger picture

If you choose to take the process through to a complete and full ending, take the last step, where you begin to envision what might be further steps and the short-term or long-term results of your actions. It is important that you not consider this as a decision-making process, but rather as a way to start to map out possible future directions. The steps are simple:

1. Ask participants to think about where the process might lead and what steps might result from the steps you have just decided.

2. List the thoughts where all participants can see them, and try to group the responses in some order or relationships. (For example, the group might envision several steps, all with the common characteristic of involving more people from the congregation.)

3. Do not list or consider questions such as "What more do we need?" or "What problems will we encounter?" These divert attention and energy away from an asset-based way of thinking and subvert the possibilities you have uncovered together earlier in the process.

A final step, prayer

Although you can start any planning session in prayer, it seems especially meaningful in an asset-based approach to wait until the end of the process before engaging in a time of meditation and prayer together. Participants will more than likely come to the end of the process with an overwhelming sense of God having blessed their time together. They will come to realize how God has visited them during their time together, and how various moments of joyful discovery were truly from the Holy Spirit.

In your prayers, do not forget to thank God for the surprises only God can give, and leave time for silence—in prayer or in meditation—to mentally review what you have come through together. Your doubts and misgivings were gradually thawed by the warmth of God's energy; you have avoided the sometimes normal processes of guilt and despair, whining and blaming; you have come to know each other better, especially for your enormous gifts and capabilities for ministry. In all of this, you have cause and will find pause for praising God. If you have the assets in your group, sing a hymn and shout "Amens" together. God has been with you, as promised!

Some final thoughts

Asset-based thinking is consonant with the message and power of the gospel. We follow a Christ and serve a God who always fulfills promises, whose word is good. And that word is always forward-looking, always focused on ministering to and with others, always purpose-driven.

At the same time, an asset-based planning approach is only one among many, and open to problems as well as possibilities. The worth of the process of asset-based planning rests on your continuing skill in trying it over and over again, in a variety of places and with a variety of people.

Asset-based planning will not cure diseases or enable anyone to walk on water, but it holds the promise of turning around negative attitudes and negative congregations. It can bring a spark of promise and hope to individuals and congregations who have planned their way into inaction, been paralyzed by analysis, or who have grown weary with the size of the mountains and walls that prevent them from accomplishing what they most want to do. Asset-based planning can also start to transform the way your congregation thinks and acts in its prioritizing of "necessary" tasks, and can help re-interpret "what must be done" so that what is done will be accomplished with capacity and joy, or it won't be done.

Chapter 2 Tool

How We Talk around Here

One way to identify your congregation's vocabulary is to gather written material from your financial stewardship programs from the past several years. Read everything over and try to characterize the writing. Are some words and phrases repeated from year to year? If so, the words may suggest habits of thought that are assumed to be true. List the repeated words.

- What have been the main motivations for giving?

- If the circumstances were described as urgent, what were the reasons for this urgency?

- Why were people asked to give or increase their giving?

- Using what you have learned, summarize the main features of your congregation's financial stewardship programs from the recent past.

- For each of the following items, choose the phrase or sentence from Column A or Column B that best describes the way stewardship is talked about in your congregation.

Column A	Column B
Our commitment	What God has given us
Offering is "taken"	Offering is "received"
Giving is nothing more than paying the church's expenses	Giving is nothing less than an act of worship
Appeals are made apologetically	Appeals are offered as opportunities to live your faith
Resources are scarce	Resources are abundant
Giving is for budget needs	Giving is for people
Financial language is predominant	Mission language is predominant
Needs are for the budget	People have needs
Increased budget reflects increased expenses, and it is a "problem"	Increased budget reflects increased ministries, and it is a "success"

- Column A indicates a budget-appeal vocabulary. Add your own budget appeal words and phrases at the end of the column.
- Column B indicates a mission-appeal vocabulary. Add your own mission appeal words and phrases at the end of the column.
- Are there words and phrases that will not be used in your congregation's stewardship effort?
- Are there words and phrases that must be used in your congregation's stewardship effort?

Chapter 3 Tool

Why Do We Have What We Have?

Bible Study

Session 1: What Do We Have?

- *Preparation for the leader:* Read chapters 1-3 of this book and look at all three sessions of this Bible study.

- *Materials:* Writing materials and Bibles, newsprint, masking tape, and markers

Opening

- Begin with prayer.

What if we have more to be grateful for than we recognize?

- In the three sessions of this Bible study, we will explore the gifts God has given us and how we use them. Before going further, answer this question: Why do you have what you have? (Write down the first thoughts that come to mind. You will not be asked to share your answer.)

Exploring Scripture

- Have volunteers read the following Bible passages:

  Psalm 23   Matthew 25:14-30
  John 1:16   1 Corinthians 1:4-9

- What has God given us? Everything! What if we have more to be grateful for than we recognize?

Our Stewardship: Managing Our Assets, copyright © Augsburg Fortress. May be reproduced for local use.

- We may be tempted to skip a step and say that the most important thing about God's gifts is how we use them, but the gifts show us the nature of God.

God's gifts in your life

- On your own, make a list of blessings or gifts that move you to prayers of thanks to God.
- You now have a list of God's gifts in your life. How complete is your list? Are more prayers of gratitude possible in your life? Save your list for the next two sessions.

God's gifts in community life

- As a group, what are you grateful for? List the blessings or gifts given to your community, congregation, and family that move you to prayers of thanks to God.
- You now have a list of God's gifts in your community life. How complete is this list? Are more prayers of gratitude possible in your community life? Save this list for the next two sessions.
- How can your congregation express gratitude to God in new ways? In groups of three or four, write a heartfelt prayer of gratitude together.

For discussion

- Is it easier to talk about what God has given us to us as individuals or in community life? Are all of the items you listed commonly understood to be gifts or blessings? If not, what are they understood to be?
- Are we fully aware of what God has given to us, to the community, congregation, and our families? When are we done realizing what God has given us? It can be a life-long effort to realize what God has given and what God is giving.

Session 2: Faithful Use

- *Materials:* writing materials and Bibles, newsprint, masking tape, and markers

Opening

- Begin with prayer.

Exploring Scripture

- Have volunteers read the following Bible passages:

  Luke 12:35-48   Romans 12:4-8

  Luke 8:4-8, 11-15   Galatians 5:22-23

How do we use God's gifts faithfully and well?

- God's purposes are worked out not only in what we have but also in our faithful use of these gifts. When we become increasingly aware of what we have, and give thanks to God for these blessings, we are ready for a second step.

- Write down your answer to this question: How do we use God's gifts faithfully and well? (You will not be asked to share your answer.)

God's gifts in your life

- Looking back at Session 1 and the list of gifts God has given you, are there any gifts you wish to add to the list?

- In what situations do you feel your gifts matter the most? When are you most sure that you are using your gifts faithfully and well?

- No one possesses all gifts. How are your gifts distinctive to you and your life? Looking at the gifts in your life, can you see what God wants for you?

God's gifts in community life

• Looking back at Session 1 and the list of gifts God has given in community life, are there any gifts you wish to add to the list?

• How do our communities use God's gifts faithfully? List ways that your community, congregation, and family use God's gifts. Then list some new ways that your communities can use God's blessings.

For discussion

• Looking at God's gifts, can we see how God wants us to use them?

Session 3: Faithful Offering

- *Materials:* writing materials and Bibles

Opening

- Begin with prayer.

Exploring Scripture

- Have volunteers read Matthew 25:31-46.
- Are God's gifts to be offered only in church or only for religious causes? In this session, we'll search out new ways to offer what God has given us.
- When we become increasingly aware of what we have, give thanks to God for these blessings, and use God's gifts faithfully and well, we are then ready for a third step.
- Write down your answer to this question: How do you offer the gifts God has entrusted to you? (You will not be asked to share your answer.)

God's gifts in your life

- Looking back at sessions 1 and 2 and the list of gifts God has given you, are there any gifts you wish to add to the list?
- When do you feel that you offer God's gifts?
- When are you most sure that you are offering your gifts faithfully and well?
- How is your knowledge of God related to what you have to give?
- Looking at what you have to give, can you see what God wants for you?

God's gifts in community life

• Looking back at Session 1 and the list of gifts God has given in community life, are there any gifts you wish to add to the list?

• How do you offer the gifts entrusted to your community, congregation, and family? Search out some new ways that these communities can offer God's blessings.

For discussion

• Looking at God's gifts, can we see how God wants us to offer them?

To end this study

• At the start of this study you wrote down an answer to this question: Why do you have what you have? How do you respond to this question today?

Why do you have what you have?

Chapter 4 Tool

Property Checklist

Our congregation has developed and follows good practices such as these:

☐ We are aware of the zoning and planning requirements of the district where our congregation is located and comply with these requirements.

☐ We meet all building-code requirements applicable to the nature and uses of our property.

☐ We have reviewed our facilities and activities for access by people with disabilities and have taken reasonable steps to provide access.

☐ We inspect our premises regularly and have programs in place to address potentially hazardous situations, such as the following:

- Snow removal and sanding or salting drives, walks, and steps are completed in a timely manner.

- Entries or other locations where people may be present are protected from falling snow and ice.

- Stairwells are well lighted and have handrails.

- Glass doors are marked so people will notice them.

- Floors are kept free of obstacles or conditions that might make people slip or trip.

- Other dangerous conditions are identified and eliminated, secured, or made subject to warnings.

- The kitchen is kept clean, old food is thrown out, and good sanitation is maintained.

- Our congregation is aware of and complies with any state or local regulations that apply to food service or sale of food.

- We are aware if there is any asbestos or lead paint on the church premises and have taken any steps that are required by law or prudence to remove it.

- Smoke detectors are provided and batteries are changed on a regular schedule.

- Fire extinguishers are provided and the staff is trained on their location and use.

❑ Other practices developed for our congregation:

Chapter 4 Tool

Liability Insurance Checklist

Our congregation has developed and follows good practices, such as these:

❑ Our insurance policies are maintained indefinitely in a central file.

❑ If we have not retained insurance policies, with the help of our agent we have reconstructed our policy coverage as much as possible.

❑ Our insurance policies are audited annually to determine the nature, amount, and sufficiency of coverage.

❑ We have designated a responsible person or committee to keep informed and current on our insurance coverage and needs, and to deal regularly with our insurance agent.

❑ Our employees and volunteers are covered individually for the same liability as the congregation (except for intentional acts, such as sexual misconduct).

❑ All of our ministry activities are insured, however separate they may be from the congregation's central activities.

❑ We read and review all of our insurance policies to be sure that they contain the coverage we think we have, and that we understand the exclusions, definitions, and endorsements.

❑ We have coverage for personal injury as well as bodily injury.

❑ We give prompt written notice to the insurer of any matters that come to our attention that could become the basis of a claim.

❏ We have adequate coverage for any motor vehicles we own.

❏ We have non-owned auto coverage to protect us in the event of liability for accidents in which an employee or volunteer is driving his or her own vehicle on congregation business.

❏ We have malpractice, professional liability, or errors and omissions coverage for all congregation ministries and activities, including counseling, that may result in damage other than by bodily injury or property damage.

❏ We have directors and officers coverage that also covers the congregation.

❏ We have adequate property damage coverage for all risks to which our property is exposed, and in sufficient amounts to cover total loss.

❏ We have fidelity bond coverage for people who handle the congregation's funds.

❏ We understand the deductible and defense costs for each of our policies.

❏ Our comprehensive general liability is not limited to accidents that occur on the premises.

❏ We have made provisions for injuries to volunteers.

❏ Other practices developed for our congregation:

Financial Assets Checklist

Handling money

Our congregation has developed and follows good practices such as these:

❑ Weekly offerings are counted immediately after the service by two unrelated people, neither of whom handles the books or writes checks.

❑ A written record of the counting is made.

❑ Funds are deposited immediately.

❑ Bills and obligations are approved before payment, and checks are signed by two people.

❑ An Audit Committee conducts an annual audit in accordance with established procedures.

❑ People with accounting training are on the Audit Committee or establish its procedures.

❑ The congregation has a fidelity bond for employees and volunteers who handle our funds.

❑ Significant sums of cash are not left in the church.

❑ All expenditures are accounted for by receipts or by written records.

Acquiring funds

Our congregation has developed and follows good practices such as these:

❑ Our congregation is aware of the reporting obligations we have to the state for ourselves or auxiliary or affiliated organizations or programs.

❑ Our congregation is aware of and obtains necessary licenses or permits for fund-raising activities.

❑ Our congregation conducts no fund-raising activities in which contributors expect some financial or material return, except with the advice of qualified counsel.

❑ Funds raised by the congregation are used only for the purpose for which they are raised.

❑ People who may be subject to undue influence are encouraged to seek independent qualified advice before making major gifts to the congregation.

❑ Donors are discouraged from attaching conditions or restrictions on gifts wherever possible.

Dealing with conditions and restrictions

Our congregation has developed and follows good practices such as these:

❑ Our congregation council is aware of, respects, and deals with as necessary conditions, restrictions, and limitations placed by the donor on assets given to the congregation.

❑ Our congregation council keeps and accounts for restricted funds and operating funds separately.

❑ Other practices developed for our congregation:

Chapter 5 Tool

Sample Program Budget

Pledged Gifts	$341,745
Non-pledged Gifts	78,836
Other	20,860
Total	$441,441

What we give together:	
Benevolence	$32,520
Mortgage	46,000
Bible Camp	1,000
	79,520
What we do together	
Worship	$103,473
Learning	54,251
Witness	48,347
Service	83,465
Nurture & Fellowship	72,385
	$361,921
Total	$441,441

In the section that follows, percentages show the percent of total dollars spent for each item across all categories. For example, youth programming is broken down this way:

Worship:	15%
Learning:	15%
Witness:	10%
Service:	10%
Nurture & Fellowship:	50%
TOTAL:	100%

Ministries

$9,365   *Worship*

Property	5%
Stewardship Education	5%
Worship and Music	40%
Christian Education	10%
Social Ministry	10%
Youth	15%

$11,574   *Learning*

Stewardship Education	25%
Finance	5%
Worship and Music	10%
Christian Education	45%
Social Ministry	5%
Youth	15%

$19,349   *Witness*

Property	30%
Stewardship Education	40%
Worship and Music	30%
Christian Education	10%
Social Ministry	15%
Witness and Outreach	40%
Youth	10%

$30,392	*Service*	
	Property	50%
	Stewardship Education	25%
	Worship and Music	15%
	Finance	90%
	Christian Education	5%
	Social Ministry	45%
	Witness and Outreach	35%
	Youth	10%

$17,670	*Nurture and Fellowship*	
	Property	15%
	Stewardship Education	5%
	Finance	5%
	Worship and Music	5%
	Christian Education	30%
	Social Ministry	25%
	Witness and Outreach	25%
	Youth	50%

Staff

This section of the program budget reflects the amount of time each position spends on worship, learning, witness, service, and nurture and fellowship. In this example, Jerry spends 80% of his time on worship-related activities and 15% on service-related activities, while Jackie's time is divided among all five categories at 20% each.

$94,108	*Worship*	
	Chris	85%
	Jerry	80%
	Louise	10%
	Anita	20%
	Miguel	30%
	Roger	30%
	Jackie	20%

$42,677   *Learning*

Jerry	5%
Louise	40%
Anita	30%
Miguel	15%
Roger	15%
Jackie	20%

$28,998   *Witness*

Louise	10%
Anita	15%
Miguel	20%
Roger	20%
Jackie	20%

$53,073   *Service*

Chris	15%
Ned	100%
Louise	5%
Anita	5%
Miguel	5%
Roger	5%
Jackie	20%

$54,715   *Nurture and Fellowship*

Jerry	15%
Louise	35%
Anita	30%
Miguel	30%
Roger	30%
Jackie	20%

Chapter 8 Tool

Sample Endowment Policy

This sample shows how one congregation set up an endowment fund. As with all legal changes, when establishing a policy such as this, check your denomination's model constitution and contact your synod or judicatory office to ensure consistency with your denomination's requirements. Also consult with the constitutional review committee for your synod or region.

I. Endowment Authorization

    A. Educate on the Needs and Benefits of an Endowment Fund

    B. Constitutional Amendment Required

        1. Appropriate notification of meeting required

        2. Prepared written amendment

            a. Recommend legal involvement

            b. Church Council to contact legal counsel

        3. Prepare draft from existing examples

            a. Obtain Council approval

            b. Legal counsel prepare final draft

    C. Create an Endowment Committee ("Committee," hereafter)

        1. Primary duties

            a. Accept funds

            b. Define disbursements

            c. Assure policy is followed

        2. Number and term of officers

            a. Five voting and two non-voting members

                 i. Non-voting are to be representatives of the Council

                ii. Voting members are to be elected by Congregation at the Annual Meeting.

                iii. Committee candidates shall be nominated by the authority of the Church Council and elected by the Congregation, responsible to the Congregation

  b. Non-voting members include a Pastor of the Congregation and the designated representative of the Church leadership.

  c. Officers (Voting members)

   i. Recording Secretary

   ii. Financial Secretary

   iii. Chairperson

   iv. Vice Chair

   v. Second Chair

  d. Committee will have three year terms to allow for rotation

   i. Inaugural committee will have staggered terms

   ii. determined by the Committee at organization

   iii. One member will serve a one year term

   iv. Two members will serve two year terms

   v. Two members will have three year terms

II. Fund Structure

 A. Objective of the Fund

  1. Provide a device for the receipt of bequests and gifts including cash, securities, real estate, life insurance, or other types of endowments.

  2. Encourage bequests and gifts of accumulated assets promoting faithful Christian stewardship, reflecting God's love, enhancing mission and outreach beyond expected and regular giving

  3. Distribute the income of the Fund annually to include:

   a. Designations by the donor

   b. Mission and outreach at large (global outreach)

   c. Community outreach and ministry (local outreach)

   d. Educational and scholarship outreach (for religious career opportunities)

 B. Fund will accept designated or undesignated gifts

  1. Undesignated bequests and gifts of less than $5,000 will not be placed in the Fund

  2. If an immediate and urgent need for an undesignated bequest or gift does not exist, the gift should be directed to the Fund

  3. The Church Council can place bequests and gifts in the Fund

 C. Investment policy

  1. The investment policy of the Fund will follow the guidelines established by our denomination.

  2. The Fund will have an initial minimum balance of $25,000

D. Distribution of funds

1. Income of the Fund will be distributed annually until the Fund reaches the sum of $100,000

2. When the Fund has moneys at or above $100,000, the income and 2 percent of the principal above $100,000 will be distributed

3. The distributions of the Fund will be distributed to each of the four designated categories (IIA.3.) in 20 percent increments each

4. The remaining20 percent Fund annual distributions will be distributed to one or more of the four designated categories, in a ratio determined by the Committee

E. Fund structure review

1. The Fund structure will be reviewed once each five years.

2. The purpose of the review will be to ensure bequests and gifts, distributions and distribution categories meet the purposes and goals of the Endowment Fund and our Church.

3. The Committee will conduct the review.